#19

McCulloch v. Maryland

When State and Federal Powers Conflict

Bonnie Pettifor and Charles E. Petit

Landmark Supreme Court Cases

Enslow Publishers, Inc.

40 Industrial Road   PO Box 38
Box 398   Aldershot
Berkeley Heights, NJ 07922   Hants GU12 6BP
USA   UK

http://www.enslow.com

Library of Congress Cataloging-in-Publication Data

Pettifor, Bonnie.
    McCulloch v. Maryland : when state and federal powers conflict /Bonnie Pettifor and
Charles E. Petit.
        p. cm. — (Landmark Supreme Court cases)
    Summary: Examines the Supreme Court case of 1819 in which the issue of state right
came to bear on banking practices of the Bank of the United States in Maryland.
    Includes bibliographical references and index.
    ISBN 0-7660-1887-3
    1. McCulloch, James W.—Trials, litigation, etc.—Juvenile literature. 2. Maryland—
Trials, litigation, etc.—Juvenile literature. 3. Bank of the United States (Baltimore,
Md.)—Trials, litigation, etc.—Juvenile literature. 4. Banks and banking, Central—Law
and legislation—United States—History—19th century—Juvenile literature. 5. Exclusive
and concurrent legislative powers—United States—History—19th century—Juvenile liter-
ature. 6. State rights—History—19th century—Juvenile literature. [1. McCulloch, James
W.—Trials, litigation, etc. 2. Maryland—Trials, litigation, etc. 3. Bank of the United
States (Baltimore, Md.)—Trials, litigation, etc. 4. Banks and banking, Central.
5. Exclusive and concurrent legislative powers. 6. State rights.] I. Title: McCulloch versus
Maryland. II. Petit, Charles E. III. Title. IV. Series.
    KF228.M318 P48   2003
    346.73'08211—dc21

                                                              2002154645

Printed in the United States of America

10 9 8 7 6 5 4 3 2 1

To Our Readers:
We have done our best to make sure that all Internet Addresses in this book were active and
appropriate when we went to press. However, the author and publisher have no control over
and assume no liability for the material available on those Internet sites or on other Web
sites they may link to. Any comments or suggestions can be sent by e-mail to
comments@enslow.com or to the address on the back cover.

Photo Credits: 1995 Historical Documents Co., 11; Collection of the Supreme
Court of the United States, p. 102; Courtesy of http://teachpol.tcnj.ed/
amer_pol_hist/thumbnail66.html, p. 60; Dover Publications, Inc., pp. 17, 47, 51,
65, 85; John Bavaro, p. 34; Library of Congress, pp. 19, 38, 42, 69; The Maryland
Historical Society, p. 7.

Cover Illustration: Richard Silverberg

Contents

1

A Visit to the Bank

One day in early May 1818, John James climbed the stairs leading to a bank in Baltimore, Maryland.

He was not going to deposit his pay or withdraw money from a personal account. Instead, Mr. James hoped to become rich from a fine he expected to collect. Ultimately, his trip up the stairs made possible a strong United States economy and a strong federal government.[1]

Mr. James met with James McCulloch, the cashier of the Bank of the United States in Baltimore. Mr. McCulloch refused to pay the fine. Mr. James went back down the steps empty-handed.[2]

James McCulloch

John James's concern was the wrongdoing he believed the Bank had committed. Later, more wrongdoing would be suspected of James McCulloch. For the three years before Mr. James's visit, James McCulloch and three other men in Baltimore had been stealing from the Bank of the United States. As the Bank's cashier, Mr. McCulloch was able to arrange loans for himself and his three friends that they never intended to repay. Eventually, the bank lost $1.4 million on these loans.

In addition, he and his friends had also broken other rules in the bank's charter.

Certain rules are set up to prevent a small group from controlling the bank. A corporation is owned and controlled by its shareholders. A shareholder owns a share, or part, of the corporation. Ordinarily, each share has one vote. For example, someone who owns ten shares has ten votes. The charter of the Bank of the United States limited each person to thirty votes, no matter how many shares he owned. To get around this rule, McCulloch and his friends registered their shares in many different names. Some were false names; others were just people who did not know they were now "shareholders." Each registration named McCulloch, or one of his friends, as the person to cast the votes for those shares. Instead of being limited to 120 votes, McCulloch and his friends had more than 4,000.[3] This gave them an unfair influence on the decisions of the Bank of the United States, including having the Bank hire McCulloch as the cashier of its Baltimore branch office.

Early Banks in the United States

The first banks in the United States began around 1780, just thirty-eight years before the *McCulloch* case. Banks also failed more often, causing more damage than they do now.

The United States still struggled to use the systems it had inherited from England. This would have been difficult enough if a dollar in South Carolina had been worth the same amount of English money as it was in Massachusetts. Unfortunately, the colonies each set their own exchange rate, ranging from five shillings to the dollar in Massachusetts to seven or more shillings per dollar elsewhere.[4]

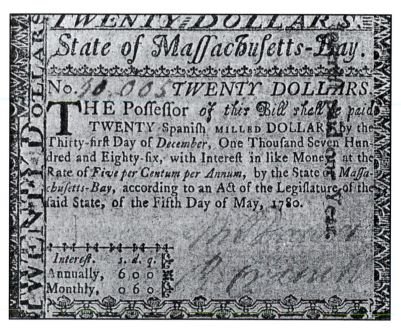

In the 1700s and 1800s, banknotes were printed by individual states or the Continental Congress.

At the time of the Revolutionary War, both the Continental Congress and the individual states issued banknotes, usually by giving a bank the right to print the money. A banknote is a piece of paper that says it is worth a certain preprinted amount of money. As time passed, these notes became more sophisticated, with many more protections against *counterfeiters* (people who illegally print their own money and try to use it instead of earning it honestly).

Banks as Businesses

The Bank of the United States was the largest corporation in the United States, and one of the largest in the world at the time.[5] It was a central bank, instead of a bank at which people keep savings and checking accounts. A *central bank* is a "bank for banks," and for the government. Its main function is to control currency, such as coins and banknotes.

Bounty-Hunting

People in many states, including Maryland, hated the Bank of the United States. For example, in February 1818, the Maryland Assembly passed a law to tax the paper used to print banknotes. The law applied only to banks in Maryland that were not *chartered,* or given permission to operate, by the state of Maryland. Only one bank in Maryland that printed banknotes was not chartered by the state of Maryland: the Bank of the United States. A coincidence? No. The tax was designed to drive the Bank of the United States out of Maryland.

Any person who gave the state evidence about banks that were not paying the taxes could earn a reward. In Maryland, this reward was half of the total amount of the tax. It was believed that the Baltimore office of the Bank of the United States had printed about 150 banknotes since the beginning of the year. Mr. James was eager to collect his share.

States' Rights and the Bank of the United States

Besides Maryland, many states were trying to keep the Bank of the United States out of their business. Other southern and western states also passed similar laws, some with even bigger fees. Georgia, North Carolina, Tennessee, Kentucky, and Ohio were some of these states. For example, Ohio set an annual fee of $50,000 for each of the two Bank of the United States offices there. Several states, such as Illinois and Indiana, made it illegal for "foreign" banks to open in their states. *Foreign* can mean from any other government, including other state governments, not just a foreign country.[6] This was another effective way to keep the Bank of the United States out of a state.

The struggle over the Bank of the United States symbolized several serious disagreements among the citizens of the young nation. The people in many states felt that they should not have to be bossed around by the federal government. After all, many remembered the fight for independence from England, which had occurred less than forty years before. Many people felt that the Bank of the United States was interfering in their freedom to conduct business as they saw fit.

Before the Constitution was ratified, each state pretty much did everything for itself. Each state had its own independent militia (army), coins, laws, roads, government, and taxes.[7] The Constitution was a compromise. Some people wanted a strong central government that would control everything in the former British colonies, somewhat like the British Parliament. Other people believed that the Revolution had been about creating "states' rights." They wanted to join the states together only tightly enough so they could protect each other. The Constitution gave each side some of what it wanted. It created a central government with many limited powers. Many other powers were left entirely to the states. For example, states still had the power to tax property, grant land, and build roads and canals.

Farmers and the Bank of the United States

Farmers did not like banks because the banks had foreclosed on loans during and after the Revolutionary War. The Revolutionary War had created great hardship for farmers; in addition to the fighting itself, the war also hurt the markets for farmers' products, like food and cotton. With so many farmers and townspeople off fighting, fewer people could buy supplies. A lot of money was spent on things for the war, too, such as muskets and gunpowder.

The war also showed the nation that the United States needed a central currency, or the same coins and paper money for everyone. It did not have one to replace the British and other currencies used by the thirteen colonies before the war. Before the Constitution was ratified in 1789, each state *minted*, or made, its own coins. States continued to control printing of paper money after ratification. This led to great confusion, for example, when farmers in Massachusetts tried to figure out whether a Connecticut dollar was worth the same amount as a Massachusetts dollar.[8]

In the 1700s, banknotes printed in one state were not always worth the same amount as banknotes printed in another state.

Business and the Bank of the United States

In contrast, shopkeepers and other businesspeople relied on banks, whether run by a state or federal government. Instead of growing things on the land, these people bought things from someone else. They either took them to a market or tried to make other things from them.

The more land a farmer owned, the wealthier he was. He did not have a great need for cash. But businesspeople depended on their services and products to make their wealth, not on how much land they owned. To get ahead, a shopkeeper had to become a better trader. A silversmith had to make more jewelry. A blacksmith had to shoe more horses. Shopkeepers and other businesspeople needed something they could give for the things they needed to buy. They also needed something they could receive for the things they sold. That something was money. The only place they could "make" money was a bank or mint.[9]

The Court System and the Bank of the United States

A major "states' rights" conflict concerned the court system. Each state had its own court system. So did the federal government. In the very early 1800s, the United States Supreme Court finally established that it had the final power to review decisions from state courts. In other words, it really was a *supreme* court.[10] It could even review some decisions on state law.[11] The Supreme Court had only begun *striking down,* or declaring invalid, state laws as "unconstitutional" in 1810.[12] Before that, the Supreme Court's only concern with state law had been whether to enforce contracts.[13]

This conflict over the court system was clear. The state governments did not like the Supreme Court's interference with state courts and state laws. A more basic conflict over the powers of Congress was less clear.

The Constitution does not just let Congress do anything it wants. Instead, it specifically assigns some powers to Congress.[14] These powers include the power to coin money; to punish counterfeiters; to declare war; and other powers. However, the Constitution does not spell out that Congress may charter a corporation such as a bank—or how to do it.

Instead, when Congress established the Bank of the United States, it relied on the last clause in the section listing its powers:

> The Congress shall have Power . . . . To make all Laws which shall be necessary and proper for carrying into Execution the [specific] Powers [granted to Congress], and all other Powers vested [given] by this Constitution in the Government of the United States, or in any Department or Officer thereof.[15]

No one in power had decided what this clause meant yet. Congress thought it had the power to charter a bank. Many citizens did not agree. This conflict was very important to James McCulloch's future.

Maryland Versus *McCulloch*

The State of Maryland took action against Mr. McCulloch and the Bank: Mr. James sued Mr. McCulloch and the Bank of the United States in Maryland's courts. The Maryland court found McCulloch and the Bank guilty. It fined him and the Bank of the United States $2,500 each.

Mr. McCulloch appealed the decision of the lower court in Maryland. The Maryland Court of Appeals denied McCulloch's appeal. So Mr. McCulloch appealed to the United States Supreme Court.[16] The Supreme Court took the appeal on a writ of error.

Could the federal government charter a bank as a corporation? Did the state of Maryland's rights outweigh the actions of the federal government?

2

The Money Game

Today, banks are essential. Banks keep track of money, save money, pay out money, and make loans. When a bank goes out of business, both the press and government investigate and discuss the matter in public for a long time. Today, banks no longer print money. Instead, they keep track of money that people have or owe on paper. Most of the "money" that banks use does not actually exist. It is only numbers in account books and computers. On the whole, the system seems to work.

Banks After the Revolutionary War

After the Revolutionary War, the new concept of paper money was fairly well established. Although many people did not really trust paper money, they usually treated it as better than no money at all. However, the young nation still had not decided who should be allowed to print and *issue*, or distribute, paper money, and when.

Alexander Hamilton was only twenty-four years old in 1779. He was an aide to General George Washington. During the war, Hamilton had tried to support an army without access to money. This struggle led him to propose a radical plan: Create a bank whose purpose was to issue paper money.[1] Over the next two years, he tirelessly wrote letters and made proposals to create a Bank of Pennsylvania in Philadelphia. By 1781, he had convinced enough people that this was a good plan. Congress chartered the Bank of North America, to be based in Philadelphia, on May 26, 1781. This bank was to be the "national bank" of the new-born United States.[2]

From the beginning, however, the Bank of North America was troubled. State governments moved quickly to support the bank. They did this by making the paper money issued by the Bank of North America "legal tender." That is, they said it must be accepted to pay any debt on the same basis as coins. Even today, the paper money minted by the United States government includes the phrase, "This note is legal tender for all debts, public and private."

The ability of the Bank of North America to print money people could use for any purpose was very important in reducing the problems caused by a short supply of coins. However, support for the Bank of North America was not wholehearted. The Massachusetts and New York legislatures

Alexander Hamilton was one of the leaders of the Federalist Party, one of the early political parties in the United States.

> **THIS NOTE IS LEGAL TENDER
> FOR ALL DEBTS, PUBLIC AND PRIVATE**

The phrase "legal tender" is still used today on paper money.

accepted the need for paper money, but objected because they did not believe Congress had the power to incorporate a bank. There was even greater hostility to the Bank of North America in its home state of Pennsylvania. This resulted from the conflicting interests of farmers and shop-keepers, as explained in Chapter 1.[3]

The real issue was trust. Farmers' past experiences with worthless money and foreclosures led them to distrust the banks. But shopkeepers needed banks every day to run their trading. The poor recordkeeping of many banks of the time made their reputations even worse.[4]

Pennsylvanian farmers succeeded in forcing the Bank of North America out of business. In 1785, they brought it under Pennsylvania law. A few short years later, they convinced the Pennsylvania legislature to revoke the Bank's charter. Several other banks had learned important lessons from the Bank of North America's experiences. The Bank of New York, which was chartered in 1791, continues to operate today.[5]

Thomas Jefferson, one of the political leaders of the new

Thomas Jefferson, the third president of the United States, is best known as the author of the Declaration of Independence.

nation, believed that a single currency was essential. He convinced the Continental Congress to adopt a radical new system for dividing the dollar into one hundred smaller units. He called these units "cents" after the Latin phrase *per cent* ("out of one hundred"). In 1785 and 1786, the Continental Congress adopted Jefferson's proposals.

The First Bank of the United States

Jefferson's efforts were important in creating trust in the dollar itself. Jefferson was not able, however, to convince skeptics that banks should be trusted. Yet, the adoption of the Constitution in 1789 created the need for a true national central bank—a kind of "united" bank for the emerging United States.

Jefferson himself was against establishing such a bank. His political opponent Alexander Hamilton proposed establishing a new Bank of the United States. Many other leaders agreed that such a bank was necessary. They were concerned, though, that Congress did not have the power to charter a bank. Hamilton convinced both the members of Congress and President Washington that Congress did have that power. The Bank of the United States was born on February 25, 1791.[6]

As mentioned in Chapter 1, this first Bank of the United States was not very popular. This was partly because people continued to distrust banks. For example, the Farmers Exchange Bank of Glocester, Rhode Island, collapsed in 1806. This event was only the first of several problems caused by poor decisions banks made in the early 1800s. For example, many banks loaned out far more money than they kept available to exchange for paper money. If someone came in with paper money and demanded that the bank give him coins in exchange, the bank would not have enough coins to make the exchange. At that time, paper money was supposed to just be a convenient substitute for coins—not a replacement for them. A lack of coins created anger and distrust when several people demanded coins at the same time.[7]

In 1811, Congress had to decide if it would renew the charter of the Bank of the United States. Leaders from both parties voted for and against renewing the Bank's charter. Some businesspeople wanted to grant the extension. Some did not. Some farmers wanted to. Some did not. Some states wanted to. Some did not. In the end, the Bank's twenty-year charter was allowed to expire.[8] The public distrust had not been overcome.

The War of 1812 and Money

The War of 1812 between the United States and England had many causes. England still resented losing the Revolutionary War thirty years before. More importantly, the United States continued to trade with France. England was angry, so it began attacking American merchant ships and making the American crews serve on English warships against France. This, in turn, made the American government angry. The War of 1812 quickly proved that the Bank of the United States' charter should have been renewed.

> Seldom have party politics been refuted [proven wrong] so fast by subsequent events. Shortly before the War of 1812 began, more than $7 million in cash had to be sent to the foreign stockholders in refund of their shares and $15 million had to be paid in [coins] to the holders of the withdrawn notes of the Bank. Thus at a critical time the available means of financing the war were severely curtailed [limited]. The local banks proved unable to fill the gap. The result was the 1814 suspension of [coin] payments and the protracted [lengthy] crisis that followed.[9]

In other words, there simply were not enough coins to pay for the war because the young nation did not have a central bank to make sure the country had what it needed.

This crisis led citizens and leaders of the new country to fully accept paper money as the American standard. The first "Treasury notes" were issued in 1815 in amounts from $5 to $100. These were official paper money issued by the United States Treasury. They could be used to purchase a "Treasury bond" over $100 that paid 7 percent interest. The bonds were very popular. This allowed the government to keep *reissuing*, or handing back out, the notes as they were turned in to buy the bonds. This kept the government from collapsing under the debts from the War of 1812.[10]

The Second Bank of the United States

The Treaty of Ghent, signed in December 1814, ended the War of 1812. Neither side had gained much through the war. Both spent money they did not have. England wanted peace so it could concentrate on defeating Napoleon Bonaparte in Europe. The United States wanted peace because the war was too expensive. England had also burned Washington in August 1814.[11] Recovery from the war was slowed by the lack of a bank to regulate the money supply. On April 10, 1816, Congress issued another twenty-year charter to form a Bank of the United States. This is usually called the "Second Bank of the United States," which became simply known as "The Bank."

Many people who had been well-known opponents of the earlier Bank of the United States now eagerly supported the new one. Congressmen John Calhoun and Henry Clay had bitterly opposed the first Bank of the United States. However, they were among the new supporters of the Bank. Daniel Webster, another leader in Congress, remained opposed to it—at least until the *McCulloch* case appeared before the Supreme Court. However, the debate was limited to whether forming this new Bank was a good idea. Hamilton's struggle to convince Congress that the Constitution gave it the power to charter a bank was not repeated. Congress simply assumed that it did have the power, without much discussion.[12]

The Second Bank of the United States faced many

challenges. It found itself in a rapidly growing economy. The *capitalization*, or initial value of stock, of the first Bank of the United States had been only $10 million. The second Bank had capitalization of $35 million. But unlike the first Bank, the second Bank had stiff competition from state-chartered banks. In addition, an economic recession in 1818 hurt the Bank.

Just like the first Bank of the United States, the second Bank of the United States had a charter for twenty years. Also like the first Bank, Congress was not in total agreement when they created the charter. To make matters worse, the second Bank was not well managed.

The manipulation of the Bank's voting stock by speculators made matters worse. The actions of the Baltimore group that included James McCulloch, as explained in Chapter 1, were especially damaging.[13]

Although the Bank was successfully issuing paper money, it had difficulty paying out coins in exchange. James McCulloch and his friends *embezzled* (a form of stealing) money from the Bank, especially its coins.

By the time James McCulloch's case came before the Supreme Court in 1819, the Bank was doing very poorly:

> [The Bank] came before the Supreme Court suing for its legality when its solvency [ability to stay in business] was in doubt. It was a half-sunk creditor, harassed and harassing. Its position was even more desperate than was known, for while its plea was being made to the Court in the name of James W.

McCulloch, he was helping himself, with his two colleagues, to its funds.[14]

James McCulloch's manipulation of the Bank's stock and loans in Baltimore eventually cost the Bank $1.5 million in 1821, almost 5 percent of the Bank's capital (net worth). Today, that $1.5 million would be worth about $1.5 billion, while 5 percent of the Federal Reserve's capital would be about $50 billion.[15] McCulloch was finally fired in May of 1820.[16]

Many leaders of the second Bank were not corrupt. Others were incompetent. In 1817, Captain William Jones was appointed president of the Bank. He had served as secretary of the Navy under President James Madison. He did not understand banking and accounting. In fact, he had declared bankruptcy shortly before he began working for the Bank! He and several of his friends ran a stock scheme very similar to the one that McCulloch and his friends were running. Captain Jones resigned in January 1820. Langdon Cheves, who became president of the Bank right after Jones, said, "I had not the faintest idea that [the Bank's] power had been so completely [exhausted] or that it had been thus unfortunately managed or grossly defrauded."[17]

Although this theft seems obviously wrong today, the Maryland courts could not handle it so easily in 1820. Maryland tried to prosecute McCulloch and his friends, but hit a roadblock almost immediately. Based on the laws Maryland had inherited from England before the

Revolution, embezzlement did not appear to be a crime! For hundreds of years, economies had been based on farming. The laws concerned themselves with the kinds of things that might go wrong on a farm. But the new economy was based on free enterprise. This had developed so quickly that the law had not caught up yet. It was clear that stealing an object from someone else was stealing. Yet, stealing the deposits in the Bank of the United States was a new twist.[18] The Bank already had the money, so was it stealing to keep it?

3

Sharing Power

McCulloch v. *Maryland* is about more than just money. The economic "climate" shows why the dispute arose. It is also important to consider why the U.S. Supreme Court made the final decision. As Chief Justice William Rehnquist said recently:

> Like so many [abstract ideas] standing alone, these tend to go in one ear and out the other when people have no regular need to [return] to such doctrine. I think that a fuller understanding of the doctrine itself may be gained by a knowledge not only of the facts of the case but also of the historical setting.[1]

The Revolutionary War was not fought by a nation, but by a group of colonies cooperating against a common enemy. That cooperation included "national" command of soldiers and ships. But each regiment of soldiers (and each ship) remained a part of an individual colony's forces. The colonies were fighting for independence from a government they believed was bossing them around too much. That is why they were not ready to immediately create another strong central government to replace the one they had just escaped.[2]

A Limited Government

Americans were not the only ones who did not like the way the English government treated the colonists. Some people in England disapproved, as well. On April 10, 1775, the lord mayor of London and several others visited King George. One of them read a statement to the king declaring "our [hatred] of the measures which have been pursued, and are now pursuing, to the oppression of our fellow subjects in America." The king was angry. He replied, "It is with . . . astonishment that I find any of my subjects capable of encouraging the rebellious [mood] which unhappily exists in some of my colonies in North America."[3] Not surprisingly, King George rejected the requests to treat the colonists with more respect. The Revolutionary War quickly broke out in Lexington, Massachusetts.

Six and a half years later, in late 1781, General Cornwallis surrendered the last large English army in the Colonies at Yorktown. The citizens of the Colonies were exhausted. Although they knew that none of the colonies were truly self-sufficient, they still did not want to form a new English government in North America. They did not want a monarch and strong central government. Their solution was a loose alliance of the colonies under the Articles of Confederation.

The Articles of Confederation continued the Continental Congress, but gave it little power. Instead, they relied on each of the new states to support each other and respect each other's laws and courts.

> The . . . States . . . enter into a firm league of friendship with each other, for their common defense, the security of their liberties, and their mutual and general welfare, binding themselves to assist each other . . . . [4]

This respect works very well when states are forced to work together (for example, by war) and when their views are the same. It does not work so well, however, when states disagree with each other. Certainly, the Articles of Confederation did not do much to help settle disputes between the states. Even though the Articles said that the states agreed to follow laws passed by Congress, Congress was powerless to do anything if a state refused.[5]

In contrast, the Articles very specifically limited the powers of Congress. About the only actions the national government could take were to manage war and negotiate with foreign countries. Individual states were expected to maintain their own armies and navies. Sometimes individual states could even have ambassadors to and from foreign countries. However, the Articles of Confederation did not authorize the national government to exchange ambassadors with foreign countries. Negotiations were allowed, but apparently only incident by incident.[6]

The Articles reinforced the concept of government *among* the states, instead of governing *of* the states. Each state had one vote in Congress, no matter how large its population was. Most of the time, a simple majority of seven of the states was enough to authorize Congress to take what little action it could. Some serious actions required more support. For example, declaring war and changing the Articles required approval of nine states out of thirteen.[7]

Many Frustrations

Citizens of the new nation discovered very quickly that the Articles of Confederation were not working very well. The Articles came into force in 1781. By 1786, there were calls for complete revision. The national economy suffered a great deal because Congress did not have the power to put to rest debts from the Revolutionary War. It could not establish a central bank to control coins and their minting. Disputes between individual states acting as *sovereigns*, or independent powers, threatened to destroy any power the Articles did have. Fortunately, in the early years after the war, the states were able to settle their differences. However, every concerned citizen could see that more serious conflicts were likely. One of those conflicts was sure to involve the banking system.[8]

Businesspeople were especially frustrated by the Articles. The different *import duties*, or taxes on goods imported into the country, in each state gave some businesspeople an unfair advantage—and made life difficult for others. Most of all, though, businesspeople were frustrated by money. There was not enough money in circulation. Money was different in appearance and value from state to state.

The Articles of Confederation gave Congress the power to mint coins, but it was never able to use that power.[9] There were too many disagreements, such as:

- Should money be based on the value of gold or silver?

- Where should coins be minted?

- Should paper money be honored for all types of payments?

Some of the individual states were so divided within themselves that the state's delegates could not agree on how to vote.[10]

Some feared that this chaos would only invite European powers to try to reconquer the United States. By 1785, many people believed that the Articles of Confederation needed to be replaced. They did not want to try to fix the Articles. They began asking for a convention at which leaders would write a completely new document to establish a strong national government.

The Constitution

The Constitutional Convention opened in Philadelphia in 1787. The delegates knew that the Articles of Confederation were failing. At the same time, they were afraid that a strong central government could oppress the people, just as England's government had a decade before. The only solution was to create something in the middle. They needed to compromise.

The Constitution was truly a radical document in its time. Even countries with elected governments allowed their governments almost unlimited power. However, the delegates of the young nation and the people they represented would not tolerate an unlimited government. But simply saying that the government may *not* do something would not have been much better. If the government grew tired of a restriction, it could just pass a bill removing the restriction. Thomas Jefferson, James Madison, and other leaders of the Constitutional Convention found a different way to keep government limited: separation of powers.

The Articles of Confederation had tried doing away with a king or queen by giving all power to Congress. Yet, it had asked Congress to do too many things while limiting its power to act. Not only must Congress pass the laws, it must also enforce them. The deep differences among the states made enforcement an impossible dream.

Three Kinds of Power

The Constitution changed the face of governments forever. It completely separated the three kinds of government power.

- Article I established a legislature, whose duty was to pass laws.

- Article II established an executive, the president, whose duty was to enforce the laws passed by the legislature.

- Article III established, for the first time in the Western world, a completely independent *judiciary*, or system of courts and judges.

Each of these branches also had the authority to keep the power of other branches in check. For example, on the one hand, the executive branch could not spend money without approval by the legislature. On the other hand, the executive branch could veto laws passed by the legislature if the laws were believed to be unwise. Neither the legislature nor the executive could dismiss judges who made unpopular decisions. In short, no one part of the government had more power than any other.[11]

In addition, the new Constitution provided that the national government must allow the states to keep playing important roles in the nation. In other words, although the Constitution made the national government's laws the

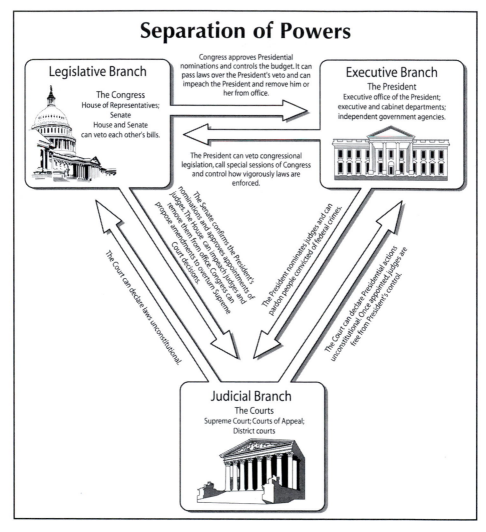

Separation of Powers

Legislative Branch

The Congress
House of Representatives;
Senate
House and Senate
can veto each other's bills.

Congress approves Presidential nominations and controls the budget. It can pass laws over the President's veto and can impeach the President and remove him or her from office.

Executive Branch

The President
Executive office of the President;
executive and cabinet departments;
independent government agencies.

The President can veto congressional legislation, call special sessions of Congress and control how vigorously laws are enforced.

The Senate confirms the President's nominations and approves appointments of judges. The House can impeach judges and remove them from office. Congress can propose amendments to overturn Supreme Court decisions.

The Court can declare laws unconstitutional.

The President nominates judges and can pardon people convicted of federal crimes.

The Court can declare Presidential actions unconstitutional. Once appointed, judges are free from President's control.

Judicial Branch

The Courts
Supreme Court; Courts of Appeal;
District courts

"supreme Law of the Land," there were many powers that the national government still left for the states.[12]

Disagreement, Then Ratification

Not everyone agreed that this new "federal" government was the best solution to the nation's problems. Many people, even some of the nation's leaders, believed that the concept of the Articles of Confederation was sound, but that the structure was wrong. The federal system proposed in the Constitution makes the national government a partner of each state. The national government "wins the argument" with disagreeing states, but only in those areas the national government is allowed to control. The people who supported this idea were called Federalists. (Later, after the Constitution was ratified, these people formed the Federalist Party to continue and expand this idea.) The Anti-Federalists were mostly in favor of a different balance. They wanted the states to be supreme. In their vision, the national government was a way to ensure that the states cooperated. The individual states would still be the nation.[13]

After the Constitution was signed, the Federalists and Anti-Federalists continued to argue back and forth in the newspapers. Each side hoped to influence the voters in the states, who still needed to ratify the Constitution. State by state, the majority of voters approved the new Constitution. It was ratified in 1788.

One of the first things the new government needed to do was appoint justices to the Supreme Court and establish courts under the Supreme Court.[14] John Jay became the first Chief Justice of the United States on October 19, 1789, and the Supreme Court began its journey toward its current role.[15]

Judicial Review

A legal system must help people resolve disagreements without violence. The judges in that system are responsible for determining the facts of a dispute. They must then apply the law to those facts and reach a result. Sometimes the law is unclear. The judge must then consider all the other laws, and decide what the law in question means.

The Supreme Court often has the final say on what a law means. When the Constitution was adopted, though, this power was not as clear to people as it is now. Article III gives the "judicial Power of the United States" to the Supreme Court and other lower courts that Congress creates to assist it. It would be up to the Supreme Court, led by the Chief Justice, for the first few years to define what "judicial power" really means. A quick look at the following case will show just how important this was—and how difficult.

Early Days of the Supreme Court

The elections in the fall of 1800 created the first of these important cases. William Marbury was promised a judgeship by the Federalist Party, which had formed around the leading Federalists. President John Adams had properly signed the commission. Unfortunately, Marbury's commission had not yet been delivered to him on the last day before the Republican president-elect (Thomas Jefferson) would take office. After President Jefferson took office, James Madison, the new secretary of state, refused to honor any of the undelivered commissions. Marbury sued to force the president to honor his commission. The decision in this case, *Marbury* v. *Madison,* established that the Supreme Court truly determined the meaning of the Constitution.[16] This also meant that the Supreme Court determined the meaning of the laws established under the Constitution.

Chief Justice John Marshall was a veteran of Virginia politics. He believed in a strong government. However, he knew that leaning too heavily in the Federalist Party's favor risked damaging the Supreme Court, especially since he had been appointed Chief Justice at the same time as Marbury had been appointed.

Chief Justice Marshall did three very important things with his opinion for the Supreme Court in *Marbury* v. *Madison.* First, he claimed the power to interpret the Constitution and the laws for the Supreme Court. This was, he said, the meaning of "judicial power." Second, he confirmed that William Marbury was entitled to take his seat. His commission had been properly signed, and neither the Constitution nor the statute authorizing the office required delivery. Delivery was merely a courtesy. This was a dangerous conclusion, however, because it could have made the Supreme Court appear to be another branch of the defeated Federalist Party.

In the face of this danger, Chief Justice Marshall found a solution that would satisfy almost everyone. He ruled that Marbury had chosen the wrong procedure. The Court did

Chief Justice John Marshall, who served on the Supreme Court for thirty-four years, is known as the "Great Chief Justice" because of his impact on the U.S. judicial system.

not have the power to force the President to honor the commission in an action filed directly in the Court. Marbury did have the right to sue in a lower court, requesting the action there. However, Chief Justice Marshall limited the power of the Supreme Court to review. The Supreme Court is not a trial court, except in lawsuits between two states or involving an ambassador. Therefore, the remedies that a trial court could impose were not available.[17]

Chief Justice Marshall's opinion had enough of something to please most people to prevent criticism that it was just a power-grab. The Federalist Party could feel that its belief in a strong, but limited, central government was correct. The Republican Party could see that the members of the Supreme Court were not just members of the Federalist Party out to improve their party's position. Instead, they were careful jurists. William Marbury could at least say that he was entitled to his commission, even if he had no way to enforce that right.[18]

Another case confirmed that the Supreme Court could review decisions by state courts when federal issues were involved in the case, and, if necessary, overrule them. These and other careful decisions by the Supreme Court quickly established it as a necessary and legitimate power. Ultimately, this would help the court decide the fate of James McCulloch.

4

The Case for
James McCulloch

Supreme Court procedure has changed a great deal since *McCulloch* v. *Maryland*. Now, almost all the lawyers' arguments are presented in *briefs*, or written arguments, to the court. The Justices and their clerks read these briefs before the lawyers actually appear. The lawyers usually get only half an hour each to argue their cases, and one lawyer speaks for each side.

In 1819, however, the lawyers did not write briefs. Instead, lawyers made their entire presentations through speeches to the court. Each side could have as many lawyers speak as it wanted. There were almost no time limits on the lawyers. The lawyers spoke for nine days, six hours each day, in *McCulloch*.

At the time of *McCulloch*, the Supreme Court employed

Henry Wheaton as its reporter. Part of his job was taking detailed notes of what the lawyers said. Then, he organized those notes and published them with the written decision of the Court.[1]

A Former Opponent

The first lawyer who spoke on behalf of James McCulloch was Daniel Webster. Mr. Webster was famous for his long but very effective speeches to the court. He was equally well known as a congressman from New Hampshire and Massachusetts.[2] Although he had originally opposed creating a second Bank of the United States, he argued in its favor in this case.

Congress Had the Power to Incorporate a Bank

On February 22, 1819, Mr. Webster began his argument by stating what he believed was the first—and most important— question that the Supreme Court must answer: "[W]hether Congress constitutionally possesses the power to incorporate a bank."[3] In simpler words, "Does Congress have the power to establish a bank as a legal corporation?"

Webster answered his own question. He pointed out that almost every session of Congress since the first in 1791 had assumed that it had the power to incorporate a bank. The president and the courts had also assumed that Congress had that power.

WEBSTER

Daniel Webster was the best-known American orator of his time.

But assuming that Congress had the power was and is not good enough. Knowing this, Webster took the next step and found two sources of Congress's power to incorporate a bank. First, he found the Necessary and Proper Clause of the Constitution:

> The Congress shall have Power . . . to make all Laws which shall be necessary and proper for carrying into Execution the [listed] Powers, and all other Powers vested [given] by this Constitution in the Government of the United States, or in any Department or Officer thereof.[4]

Another clause gives Congress the power to regulate money.[5]

Webster seems to be saying that incorporating a bank to regulate, mint, and print money is a "necessary and proper" law.[6] After all, other nations that used banknotes had incorporated banks to handle all the chores of dealing with the money supply. For example, England had incorporated the Bank of England in the late 1600s.[7]

Webster also made a less obvious argument: that the power to act at all must mean the power to select *how* to act. For example, the Constitution gives Congress the powers to maintain a navy and an army and to declare war.[8] Webster argued that giving Congress those powers also means that Congress has the power to take other actions to support them. To maintain a navy, Congress must be able to raise money to pay for it. It must also be able to make other related decisions, such as to buy new technology. Steam-powered warships had certainly not been on the minds of the members of the Constitutional Convention thirty years before. Yet, the steam-powered warship was invented around 1816 and widely discussed in newspapers. It would be ridiculous to believe that giving Congress the general power to maintain a navy did not also give the power to keep it competitive with other nations.[9]

This simple example allowed Webster to explain the difference between a power itself and the means used to exercise that power. His argument echoed one of the major arguments at the Constitutional Convention: How much must the young nation limit the powers and actions of the central government? Article I, Section 8 of the Constitution gives Congress eighteen different kinds of powers, including the "necessary and proper" powers in the last clause. These powers limit the reach of government's authority. These limits were made very clear in the Tenth Amendment, ratified in 1791. The Tenth Amendment clearly kept every power not otherwise granted to the federal government for the states and the citizens.[10]

Webster ended this part of his argument by putting the burden on the other side: those challenging whether a disputed act of Congress was constitutional. Webster seems to think so because Congress carefully considers each law before it votes on it. At the same time, Congress must also consider whether the proposed law would be within its powers. If Congress believes this at first, then the side that believes the law is unconstitutional must prove that it is unconstitutional. It is not the government's burden to prove itself to be right.[11]

States Did Not Have the Power to Tax the Bank

Then Webster asked: If Congress has the power to charter a bank, does a state have the power to tax that bank? Webster said it did not. First, he reminded the Supreme Court that the Constitution takes priority over anything done by individual states. This includes acts of Congress that fall within the authority granted by the Constitution.[12]

Next, he linked this issue with one of the main issues that led to the Revolutionary War: unlimited powers to tax. Webster said that the Constitution does not allow anyone to say, "tax this much, but no more." As he had pointed out earlier in his argument, the Constitution is about powers, not specific issues. He concluded that states cannot tax the federal government or organizations created by the federal government, because the "power to tax is the power to destroy." If the states could tax federal organizations, they could make the taxes so high that the organization could not function. In reality, this would allow the states to overrule federal legislation. The Maryland law about banknotes was exactly this kind of tax: a tax intended to destroy. Webster concluded that the tax was therefore invalid.[13]

The Attorney General

The next lawyer to speak after Mr. Webster was Joseph Hopkinson, on behalf of the state of Maryland (see Chapter 5). Mr. Hopkinson was followed by William Wirt, the attorney general of the United States. Mr. Wirt had begun his service as attorney general in 1817, and would eventually argue 174 cases before the Supreme Court.[14] His argument reinforced Mr. Webster's.

To begin, Mr. Wirt emphasized that it would be inappropriate to remove a power from Congress that it had exercised for nearly thirty years. He also said that granting power "without the means to use it is a nullity [meaningless action]." This means that a power without any way to use it means nothing.[15] This echoed Mr. Webster's argument that granting a power must also grant the ways to use it.

The Constitution Versus the Law

Then Mr. Wirt discussed the difference between the Constitution and a law. He said that the Constitution is a guide to permanent features of the government. It is purposely vague in the powers it grants, because the Framers (writers) of the Constitution knew that they could not think of everything that the nation might encounter in the future.

However, the Constitution is quite specific in the powers it forbids. On the one hand, it grants Congress the power "to provide and maintain a Navy." On the other hand, it specifically prohibits bills of attainder. A *bill of attainder* is

At the time of *McCulloch* v. *Maryland*, William Wirt was attorney general of the United States.

an act that punishes a person or organization by legislation (not after a court trial), or punishes a guilty person's family and descendants.[16] Mr. Wirt's point is that the Constitution is flexible in allowing Congress to take some actions, but rigid in prohibiting others. Chartering a bank or corporation is not specifically prohibited. Therefore, such a charter must be constitutional if it is being used to support one of the powers granted to Congress.[17]

The States May Not Undo a Federal Action

Mr. Wirt also discussed the right of states to tax a corporation chartered by Congress. He believed that such a tax would be unconstitutional, even under the Tenth Amendment. He accepted that the Tenth Amendment does give the states the powers not granted to the federal government. However, he said that this cannot mean that the states have powers to undo actions by the federal government. The amendment does not say that.

Most importantly, the Supremacy Clause of the Tenth Amendment says the following:

> This Constitution, and the Laws of the United States which shall be made in [following it]; . . . under the Authority of the United States, shall be the supreme Law of the Land; and the Judges in every State shall be bound thereby, any Thing in the Constitution or Laws of any State to the Contrary notwithstanding [no matter what the laws of a state are].[18]

This means that once Congress acts, the states may not

pass laws that contradict Congress's laws. This applies as long as what Congress did is constitutional in the first place. It also means that state court judges cannot enforce their own state's laws if they would contradict the actions of the federal government.

The Power to Incorporate is Constitutional

Mr. Wirt's argument cleverly reduced the case to only one question: Was the act of chartering the Bank of the United States constitutional? If it was, then the states may take no action to harm that charter. As Mr. Webster had pointed out, taxing the Bank would have been harmful. Maryland's particular tax was passed specifically to harm the Bank and drive it out of Maryland.

Mr. Wirt also appealed to the personal power of the Supreme Court Justices. Mr. Webster had mentioned only taxing corporations chartered by Congress. He felt this showed that this was potentially the power to destroy those corporations. Mr. Wirt took this argument one small step further. He said that if the states can tax corporations chartered by the United States, they can also tax anything else established by the United States. Specifically, Mr. Wirt charged that allowing the states to tax the Bank would also allow them to tax federal courts.[19]

Although Mr. Wirt did not say so, everyone in the courtroom—especially the Justices—knew that the states were even more hostile toward the federal courts than they were toward the Bank of the United States. The Supreme Court had decided several cases in ways that restricted states' power. For example, the Court had ruled that people who purchased land from the English government had the right to the land, even if a state later seized that land during the Revolutionary War. The Court said that the Constitution clearly prohibited states from interfering with contracts, and that buying land is nothing more than a contract.[20]

The Eleventh Amendment was adopted in 1798 to prevent federal courts from hearing many cases against the states. This also showed the states' hostility toward federal courts.[21]

The Marylander

After another of Maryland's lawyers spoke, William Pinkney made the last speech defending the Bank. Pinkney was almost as famous as Daniel Webster. He had just finished serving as attorney general of the United States. Ironically, his home state was Maryland. His defense of the Bank became his most famous case.[22]

Mr. Pinkney began by agreeing with Mr. Webster and Mr. Wirt that the Constitution clearly allowed Congress to charter corporations to support its specific powers. He pointed out that many of the same people who voted for the first Bank of the United States also participated in writing the Constitution.

Next, Pinkney discussed the history of corporations.

William Pinkney, who had just finished serving as attorney general under President James Madison, made the last speech defending the Bank.

Corporations were not invented in the United States. Instead, they came to the United States from English law, which had modified a 2,000-year-old Roman law. Corporations in England and elsewhere in Europe did not require government approval at all. Mr. Pinkney said that this means that corporations are clearly not something just for sovereigns. This argument refutes the "states' rights" position that the individual states are sovereigns, not the federal government. In this way, Mr. Pinkney also showed that a corporation is an ordinary and necessary thing that the states cannot deny the federal government.[23]

Protecting the Constitution

Then Mr. Pinkney discussed what "necessary" means. This makes the Necessary and Proper Clause the most important clause, because it seems to grant Congress the right to do what it needs to, to implement its other powers.[24] Mr. Pinkney gave a very flexible meaning. It does not mean there may be no other way to do what Congress wants to do. Instead, it means that Congress can decide the best way to do something for itself, as long as it follows the rest of the Constitution.[25]

Pinkney went on to support the arguments already made by Mr. Webster and Mr. Wirt: States could not tax a corporation chartered by Congress. He said:

> There is a [clear contradiction] between the power of Maryland to tax, and the power of congress to preserve,

this institution. A power to build up what another may pull down at pleasure, is a power which may provoke a smile, but can do nothing else. . . . Whenever the local councils of Maryland will it, the bank must be expelled from that State. A right to tax without limit or control, is essentially a power to destroy. If one national institution may be destroyed in this manner, all may be destroyed in the same manner.[26]

Mr. Pinkney emphasized that allowing the individual states to overrule federal acts would destroy the Constitution. He did not need to remind the Supreme Court of the chaos that occurred under the Articles of Confederation between 1781 and 1789. If Congress decided to tax state banks itself, it did so through the states' own representatives. Allowing each state a veto over national legislation would not meet the goals of the Constitution. This would be true, even if all the other states had agreed to it.[27]

Throughout the argument, all the Bank's lawyers referred to the Bank and its powers. James McCulloch was barely mentioned, except as an officer of the Bank. As shown in the next chapter, Maryland's lawyers also paid little attention to James McCulloch. The case remained in McCulloch's name because he had been fined. However, the lawyers ignored him personally during the nine days of arguments.

The Fine Must Be Cancelled

As its capable lawyers had argued, the Bank believed that the Supreme Court needed to answer two questions. The Bank's lawyers said that the act chartering the Bank was constitutional, and that the states did not have the power to tax (and so destroy) the Bank. Maryland did not have the power to tax the Bank. The fine against James McCulloch and the Bank must be cancelled.

5

The Case for Maryland

Maryland's arguments against the Bank came from a completely different perspective than the Bank's.

Joseph Hopkinson

First, Joseph Hopkinson opened his presentation with his own three questions for the Supreme Court to consider:

1. [Does] Congress [have] a constitutional power to incorporate the Bank of the United States?

2. Granting this power to congress, [does this] bank, [on] its own authority, [have] a right to establish its branches in the several states?

3. Can the bank, and its branches . . . claim to be exempt from the ordinary and equal taxation of property, as assessed in the states in which they are placed?[1]

The second question was especially important to Maryland, because Maryland's goal was to force the Bank out of the state.

Congress Did Not Have the Power to Incorporate the Bank

Mr. Hopkinson began by disagreeing with Mr. Webster's claim that Congress had the power to charter a corporation. The Constitution certainly does not directly authorize Congress to charter a corporation.[2] Mr. Hopkinson did admit that the Constitution might imply some powers it did not state explicitly. He questioned, however, whether these implications are necessarily permanent. Specifically, even if Congress had had the power to charter a bank corporation in 1791, the power would expire when it was no longer necessary. Mr. Hopkinson claimed that the Supreme Court had answered that question only a few months ago, in a case involving bankruptcies. To say this, though, was a big stretch by Mr. Hopkinson.

In that case, a New York law had changed how a *debtor,* or someone who owes money, could *discharge,* or get rid of, his debts in bankruptcy. However, the Constitution gives Congress exclusive power over bankruptcy.[3] The Supreme Court ruled that this New York law was invalid. The Court also made a minor remark that powers were not always permanent. They meant this remark only regarding bankruptcies and the powers courts needed to administer them.[4]

Mr. Hopkinson pointed out that public banks were now able to perform all of the functions within Congress's power that might have made the first Bank of the United States "necessary" in 1791. He reasoned that this meant that the second Bank of the United States was not necessary *now*. Therefore, this issue fell outside the Necessary and Proper Clause's grant of power to Congress. After all, state-chartered banks were providing all of the services needed by business-people. Because the other banks made action by *Congress* to charter a bank unnecessary, the Necessary and Proper Clause would not grant Congress the right to make such a charter.[5]

Congress Could Not Establish Branches of the Bank

The second question seems much more technical. "Granting this power to congress, [does this] bank, [on] its own authority, [have] a right to establish its branches in the several states?" Mr. Hopkinson admitted that the Bank of the United States' charter specifically allowed it to open branches. However, he questioned whether the Bank could open branches in the states without approval by Congress and the states, no matter what its charter said. This argument asks for an even stricter definition of "necessary and proper" than the chartering of the Bank. Mr. Hopkinson meant that, in his view, whether or not the act is within Congress's power is just the starting point. He argued that

Congress cannot charter a bank to do something that it could not do directly itself. He said that the Constitution does not allow Congress to establish branches of a corporation in the states, so Congress cannot charter a bank to open the branches for it.[6]

Mr. Hopkinson also argued that the Bank itself could not decide to open a branch in a state. If Congress has the power to do anything that is "necessary and proper," only Congress can decide what is necessary and proper. This argument is another restriction on the meaning of "necessary and proper."[7]

States' Rights—Again

Altogether, Joseph Hopkinson's arguments on Congress's power to charter the Bank and allow it to decide how to operate focused on two principles of "states' rights." First, he wanted to deny Congress all powers not spelled out by the Constitution. Second, if the Supreme Court decided that Congress has some implied powers, he wanted to force Congress to make every single decision on how to use those powers. This argument is usually called the *nondelegation doctrine.* This means that Congress cannot give its powers to anyone else (such as the Bank of the United States), because the Constitution gives those powers only to Congress. Applying the nondelegation doctrine as harshly as Mr. Hopkinson proposed would keep Congress from chartering banks and opening branch offices. Of course, this is exactly what Maryland wanted.

States Could Tax the Bank

Then Mr. Hopkinson turned to the remaining question—whether Maryland could tax the Bank:

> As this overwhelming invasion of State sovereignty is not warranted by any express clause or grant in the constitution, and never was imagined by any state that adopted and ratified that constitution, it will be conceded, that it must be found to be *necessarily and* [permanently] connected with the power to establish the bank, or it must be repelled.[8]

In plainer words, Mr. Hopkinson was saying that the chartering of the Bank was a violation of states' rights. It was not supported by the Constitution the states thought they were voting for in 1789. It must be decided now and forever whether Congress could establish a Bank.

Then, Mr. Hopkinson argued from this general principle that the Bank of the United States cannot be exempt from all state taxation. If it cannot be exempt from all state taxation, then he stated that this particular tax must be valid. It must be paid.

Mr. Hopkinson compared the Bank with state-chartered banks, pointing out that their operation was almost the same. They each had investors, officers, and stock. They did very much the same things. The only real difference was that the Bank was chartered by Congress, not the states. He argued that this difference was not enough to justify exempting the Bank from a state's most important power: the power to raise money by taxation.[9]

Next, Mr. Hopkinson discussed a different kind of "fairness." He pointed out that the federal government taxed state-chartered banks. Then he said that, since the states were independent sovereigns, they must be able to do to the federal government what the federal government did to the states. He cited one of the most important of *The Federalist* papers to support this argument. This collection of essays attempts to reassure the states that the Constitution does not take away states' powers to tax and give them exclusively to the federal government.[10] (This was one tool the supporters of the Constitution used to get the voters in each state to vote to accept a national Constitution.) Joseph Hopkinson said this means that the states have the power to choose how

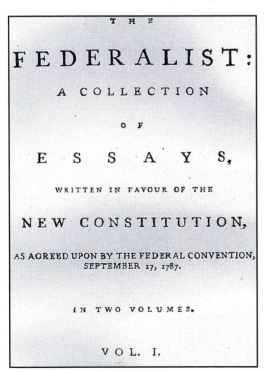

THE

FEDERALIST:

A COLLECTION

OF

ESSAYS,

WRITTEN IN FAVOUR OF THE

NEW CONSTITUTION,

AS AGREED UPON BY THE FEDERAL CONVENTION, SEPTEMBER 17, 1787.

IN TWO VOLUMES.

VOL. I.

The Federalist papers are a collection of essays written in the 1780s by Alexander Hamilton, John Jay, and James Madison. These essays were written to gather support for the proposed Constitution of the United States.

to run their own tax systems, except when the Constitution specifically limits their choices. The Constitution says that states may not tax imports and exports or ships based on their size or the weight of their cargo. It leaves states free to impose any other tax they wish, he claimed.[11]

Mr. Hopkinson finished by claiming that simply because a power to tax exists, it did not mean that the states would use taxes to keep the federal government from taking actions. For example, no state would tax a warship about to leave port, or ammunition for the army about to march off to war.[12] At first, this last argument sounds convincing. After all, the states agreed to work together in forming the Constitution. Surely they would continue to do so. However, Mr. Hopkinson's examples are exactly the extremes that he warned should not guide the Supreme Court's opinion. Maryland's attempts to tax the Bank are exactly what he argued the states would not do: impose a state tax because they disagreed with a national policy.

Robert Jones

The next speaker for the state of Maryland was Robert Jones, a Baltimore lawyer. His arguments were even more in support of "states' rights" than Mr. Hopkinson's. He said that the Constitution had not been made by the people of the nation acting together as a whole, but by the people of each state acting as states. The Constitution gave the federal government only the powers the states were willing to give up. Since the states had kept the power to charter banks, they had not given it up to the federal government. So chartering the Bank was not a power the states had given to Congress.[13]

Mr. Jones quickly moved on to whether chartering a bank is actually implied in the Constitution:

> For example, the power of coining money implies the power of establishing a mint. [I]t does not imply the power of establishing a great banking corporation, branching out into every district of the country, and [flooding it with] paper-money.[14]

This is a variation of Mr. Hopkinson's argument that "necessary and proper" is a very narrow term. Mr. Jones focused on the simple language of the Constitution's grant of the power "to coin Money, regulate the Value thereof, and of foreign Coin."[15] He said that this does not include paper money, that "coin Money" refers only to coins. Therefore, since the states had not given the power to print paper money to Congress, that must mean that the states kept that power for themselves.

Mr. Jones also relied on a very *literal*, or word-for-word, reading of the Necessary and Proper Clause to argue that this clause did not extend Congress's powers. He pointed out that the clause says "necessary *and* proper," not "necessary *or* proper." He said that this is the only way to both acknowledge that the Constitutional establishes a government of limited powers and be true to the dictionary meanings of the words "necessary" and "proper."[16] He reminded the Court that the Tenth Amendment very clearly spelled out that gave all powers are reserved to the people and the states that the Constitution did not give to the federal government.[17] Mr. Jones meant that a "power" that is not both "necessary" and "proper" under the strictest definitions in the dictionary belongs to the states, not to Congress. Most dictionaries today, and even dictionaries of that time, had more than one meaning for many words. For example, one current dictionary lists nine different definitions of "necessary" and fourteen of "proper."[18] Thus, Mr. Jones's argument would allow an opponent to pick a different, and probably irrelevant, definition to defeat an act of Congress.

Next, Mr. Jones discussed whether Maryland could tax the Bank, if somehow the Bank's charter was constitutional. Once again, he adopted a very literal reading of the Constitution. He repeated Mr. Hopkinson's statement that the only restrictions on states' powers to tax concerned imports, exports, and tonnage [weight].[19] Therefore, because the Constitution does not restrict the states' ability to impose any other kind of tax, the states must have the power to decide what to tax for themselves.[20]

Mr. Jones also supported Mr. Hopkinson's argument that the states and the federal government are equal powers.[21] (Neither Mr. Hopkinson nor Mr. Jones even referred to the Supremacy Clause in Article VI, as Mr. Webster had.)[22] Their position stayed based on their theory that the federal government is just a way for the states to cooperate and do things that they could not do separately.

The Attorney General of Maryland

Luther Martin, the attorney general of Maryland, spoke last for the State of Maryland. He began by summarizing and repeating Mr. Hopkinson's remarks on the limited powers of the federal government.[23] He also agreed with Mr. Hopkinson's remarks on the states' powers to tax.

He took this a step further by claiming that the Constitution did not give the federal government the power to "withdraw any part of the property within the state from the grasp of taxation."[24] In other words, the federal government could not protect one type of property from being taxed by a state. Martin said that it seemed that what was unfair was that something created by Congress was not "property within the state."

Martin's argument becomes clear under the theory that the Constitution is just for encouraging cooperation among the independent states. In real terms, this meant that everything the federal government "owned" was the property of the states. Anything that happened to come within the lines on the map that define a state was, therefore, "property within the state." Mr. Martin excluded the courts and customs stations from this argument by saying that courts and customs stations are not "property" at all.[25]

Luther Martin was attorney general of Maryland at the time of *McCulloch* v. *Maryland.*

The Fine Must Be Enforced

All arguments combined, the state of Maryland presented two different reasons for fining James McCulloch. Its lawyers all argued that the power to charter a bank does not appear in the Constitution, so Congress does not have that power. Even if chartering a bank is somehow an "implied power," the second Bank of the United States was not "necessary and proper" by 1816. This was, they claimed, because state-chartered banks did the same things just as well. This position assumes that the federal government is nothing more than an agreement among the states. This extreme "states' rights" argument seems weak, however, in light of the Supremacy Clause. The Supreme Court's decisions had affirmed its power to review state court decisions that concern federal law.[26]

Maryland also argued that the minimal restrictions on state taxes found in the Constitution are the only restrictions on state taxes. These arguments are based on an understandable—but mistaken—idea: If a state can impose some kind of tax on the Bank, it can impose any kind of tax that it wants to impose. However, Maryland's tax on banknotes is hardly an "ordinary and equal taxation of property." It is not a tax on property at all, but a tax on an operation. In addition, it is not "ordinary," as it applies to only one specialized kind of business. It is not "equal," as it discriminates against banks not chartered by the State of Maryland.

This dispute highlights two of the major theories on

how to interpret the Constitution. The two theories are in direct conflict with each other:

1. Maryland argued that the literal language of the Constitution and the original intentions of the people who wrote it and the states that voted for it must control its meaning. This theory is called "original intent."

2. The federal government, especially through Mr. Pinkney, argued that a "functional" theory said that the Constitution should not be limited to its literal language. Instead, it should define a broad set of functions that the federal government may or may not perform.

Although the Supreme Court would not need to say which theory it believed was correct, its opinion would answer that question.[27]

6

The Decision

After nine days of arguments by the lawyers, the Supreme Court needed to make its decision. Chief Justice John Marshall would guide the Court toward that decision.

Chief Justice John Marshall

Chief Justice John Marshall was born in Germantown, Virginia, on September 24, 1755. He was the oldest of fifteen children. The Marshall family was quite wealthy. They also had many friends and relatives in other important Virginian families—the Lees, the Washingtons, the Jeffersons, and the Randolphs. Although John Marshall had very little formal schooling, he served as an officer in the Revolutionary War. After the war, he returned home to take three months of law classes from George Wythe, founder of the law school at the College of William and Mary in

Williamsburg, Virginia.[1] In January 1783, he married Polly Ambler in Richmond, Virginia, as he began a career as a lawyer.[2]

Marshall quickly established a reputation as a smart and effective lawyer who was very polite and easy to talk to. He served as an ambassador and as secretary of state for President John Adams in the late 1790s. One of Adams's last acts as president was to appoint John Marshall as Chief Justice.[3] As current Chief Justice William Rehnquist said recently, "Even in his own lifetime [Marshall's] accomplishments as Chief Justice made such a public impression that John Adams in his retirement would say, 'John Marshall was my gift to the American people.'"[4]

Many scholars credit John Marshall with creating what is now the Supreme Court. For example, he began the practice of giving a joint written opinion after taking time to think about the issues raised by the lawyers. The English practice in place when he became Chief Justice forced each justice to give an individual opinion immediately after the lawyers finished arguing. Because this was long before the time of tape

John Marshall was instrumental in creating what is now the Supreme Court.

recorders, it made it hard to know if they were remembering the arguments accurately. Marshall's method made the rulings officially come from the Supreme Court, not from an individual judge.[5]

Not everyone liked Marshall, however. Thomas Jefferson, who was president right after John Adams, hated him intensely. Although they were both Virginians, they had very different political philosophies. These differences became very clear in the dispute over Adams's appointment of federal judges at the end of his term (see Chapter 3). Jefferson's Republican party was outraged. *Marbury* v. *Madison* affirmed the Supreme Court's power to say what the Constitution means while making it almost impossible for the Republicans to attack the Court.[6] This was because both sides had gotten most of what they wanted. Jefferson continued to hate Marshall.

The Power to Create

Marshall's early decisions on the Constitution and the powers of the Supreme Court laid the foundation for settling the dispute in *McCulloch*. By that time, almost everyone accepted that the Supreme Court had the power to review any act of Congress, or of the states, to see if it was constitutional.[7] Although the lawyers had tried to divide the case into three different questions, those questions related to two basic issues:

1. Does the Constitution include powers (and authorize actions) not spelled out that allow the federal government to support the powers it clearly does have?

2. May a state tax a corporation or other organization that has a federal charter?

The Court's answers to these questions would help determine the future of the United States. If it decided that the Constitution does not include powers that would allow Congress to charter the Bank of the United States, the Bank would immediately stop existing. This would have caused chaos among the Bank's investors. It would also have made it hard to regulate the money supply and stop counterfeiting.

In some ways, the Court's answer to the second question would be just as important. If the Supreme Court decided that Congress had the power to charter the Bank, but allowed individual states to tax it out of existence, Congress would be unable to act on behalf of the nation whenever any single state disagreed with that action. The Framers of the Constitution, however, were thinking of uniform national laws from the federal government.

Considering the Two Sides

Marshall delivered his opinion on March 7, 1819.[8] He began by pointing out that each side claimed that the other side's law was unconstitutional:

- Maryland claimed that the law chartering the Bank of the United States was unconstitutional.

- The Bank and James McCulloch claimed that the Maryland law taxing the Bank was unconstitutional.

Marshall said that these questions "must be decided peacefully, or remain a source of hostile legislation, perhaps, of hostility of a still more serious nature . . . . [To] the Supreme Court of the United States has the constitution of our country [given] this important duty."[9] In other words, if the Supreme Court did not resolve the dispute, the states and federal government could easily become more and more hostile toward each other. This could possibly lead to a civil war.

Next, Marshall considered the question of Congress's power to charter the Bank. He agreed with Daniel Webster's argument that, at least historically, this question had already been answered. The first Bank of the United States was chartered in 1791 by many of the same men who wrote the Constitution. These men had carefully considered the constitutionality of the charter before passing it. Clearly, they had been persuaded that the charter was constitutional by Alexander Hamilton—another of the men who helped write the Constitution. Marshall acknowledged that a longstanding practice could still be found to be faulty, but emphasized that the tradition deserved great weight in reaching his decision.[10]

Maryland, however, had argued that the Constitution was a *compact,* or agreement, among the states. Therefore, states had the final word on the extent of the powers they granted to Congress in the Constitution. Marshall squashed this argument by noting that the various state delegations to the Constitutional Convention had been chosen not directly by the state governments, but by other means. Members of the Convention were chosen individually, not by state governments. The states had ratified the Constitution as states, based on a popular vote in the state. He also discounted the fact that it had been states that sent delegations, because there had been no alternative. The Constitutional Convention was not a result of "compounding the American people into one common mass." That did not, however, force the opposite conclusion—that the only things that mattered at the Convention were the states.[11]

Then Marshall said that it was clear that, whatever its powers are, the federal government is "supreme within its sphere of action." Though limited in total power, it is unlimited when it has been granted powers. Marshall did not rely upon "original intent," or the opinions of individual leaders at the time the Constitution was adopted. Instead, he quoted the Supremacy Clause in Article VI, which makes the Constitution the "supreme law of the land," saying that it settled the argument.[12] This response was intended to silence the protests of those (for example, Maryland) who claimed that the states somehow kept ultimate control. Whether it was the states themselves or their citizens who approved the Constitution, the Supremacy Clause was part of what was approved.

The Tricky Part

Marshall's opinion had now set the stage for considering the hardest part of the problem. He found that the Constitution does grant implied (those not spelled out clearly) powers, because the Tenth Amendment does not negate, or cancel, them.[13] The master stroke was the way he distinguished interpreting a law from the general principles and grants of power found in the Constitution. He gently reminded the lawyers that "we must never forget, that it is *a constitution* we are expounding [interpreting]."[14] This statement is a natural result of agreeing that the Supreme Court must make these decisions. The Court has the power to interpret the Constitution. Therefore, if it says that the Constitution must be interpreted using different rules than it would use to interpret a law, then there is no room for further argument.

Chartering a Bank

The decision Marshall, and so the Court, would reach was now clear: He wrote that Congress had the power to charter the Bank of the United States. He had laid out his argument so that there was almost no way to reach a different answer. Since the Constitution is about general grants of power, it is only logical that granting the power also grants the ordinary means to execute the power. Including a corporation in this was within Congress's ability to act. Congress has legislative power. Corporations are recognized by sovereign

74

governments, and the power to create them belongs to sovereign governments. The same is true of legislation, though. Therefore, Congress had the power to charter a corporation to exercise its undoubted power to regulate money.

The Necessary and Proper Clause reinforces this position, Marshall said. So do several other powers that nobody at that time denied Congress had. For example, if Congress can create post offices, it can create the means to do so. In other words, Congress is a legislative body, not the entire government. It may apply its own judgment to how, and when, to exercise its powers.[15]

Establishing Branches

But can the corporation establish branches? This last aspect of the power question gave Marshall an opportunity to make clear that the Necessary and Proper Clause had a very broad scope. He did so by looking carefully not just at the words "necessary" and "proper" but also at the entire phrase in which they appear. Congress is granted the power to "make all laws which shall be necessary and proper to carry into execution" the other powers it has been granted. The Necessary and Proper Clause is in section 8 of Article I, which grants powers to Congress, not section 9, which restricts them. So, the Necessary and Proper Clause must be a power in itself: the power to choose the means to exercise its powers. The words cannot be read one by one, but must be read together.

In turn, this supports and affirms the Bank's right to open branches wherever it believes it must in order to carry out Congress's directions. The reasoning is much the same—if Congress can choose to implement its power to regulate money by chartering a bank corporation, the corporation in turn must be able to choose how to operate so it can perform its mission of regulating money for the whole nation. Naturally, this requires branches to accept deposits, issue banknotes, and carry on the other business of banking where the people need a bank—which is everywhere.[16]

The Power to Destroy

Then, Chief Justice Marshall considered whether Maryland had the right to tax the branches. He approved the argument made by William Pinkney on behalf of the Bank. Marshall agreed that it would make no sense to allow the state the power to destroy actions taken by the federal government to implement the federal government's powers. He also tied this logical argument back into the Supremacy Clause. Allowing the state such power to destroy, or to regulate, federal efforts would be "repugnant" (offensive and improper). It would also violate the Supremacy Clause, which confirms that federal powers overrule any opposition from the states. When the federal government is constitutionally exercising its powers, the states may not interfere. Taxing the bank would interfere with its operation. Marshall agreed that the heavy taxes many states would impose would destroy it.[17]

The Question of States' Rights

Finally, Chief Justice Marshall returned to the theme of "sovereignty." He said that this also denies states the power to tax federal corporations. The sovereign powers of the federal government come from the same source as the sovereign powers of the states themselves—from the people. The federal government was not created by the states. It did not have to follow the states' wishes—only the people's wishes. The people chose to create both the states and the federal government. That must mean, even without the Supremacy Clause, that the collective federal government can overrule the individual states. The Supremacy Clause makes this clear.[18]

A Groundbreaking Opinion

The judgment of the Supreme Court was unanimous. Congress did have the power to charter the Bank of the United States. In turn, the Bank had the power to establish branches so it could fulfill the mission Congress assigned. However, Maryland did not have the power to interfere by taxing the Bank. Therefore, the fine imposed on the Bank and James McCulloch by the Maryland courts was invalid.[19]

The opinion in *McCulloch* v. *Maryland* looks very different from an opinion that the Supreme Court might issue today. Today, the arguments of the lawyers are not printed along with the opinion. Even more importantly, a Supreme Court decision today will *cite*, or rely on as a reference, many other cases that the Court has previously decided—often *McCulloch* itself. *McCulloch* is one of the last opinions issued by the Court that does not rely on citations to previous cases. Instead, the Court relied almost entirely on the text of the Constitution and careful logic.

Of course, there were not as many previous cases to draw on then as there are now. Now the Court's opinions fill over five hundred very thick books, adding three to five more every year!

7

The Decision and the Money System

McCulloch v. *Maryland* answered many questions about banking, money, and taxes in the United States—at least for that time.[1] Today, the Bank of the United States no longer exists. The Federal Reserve Bank of the United States now controls the money supply. Money is actually printed and minted by the U. S. Department of the Treasury. Money is certainly still important, though! Today, most money is just numbers in an account book. For example, in 1999, the U.S. economy was "worth" about $4 trillion. However, the total amount of paper money and coins was much less than one trillion dollars.[2]

The Bank of the United States

Just like the first Bank of the United States, the second Bank of the United States had a charter for twenty years. Also like the first Bank, not every Congressman agreed completely about creating the charter. As discussed earlier, the second Bank was not well managed. James McCulloch was not an honest bank official, either. His manipulation of the Bank's stock and loans in Baltimore eventually cost the Bank a lot of money. He was fired as cashier in May of 1820.[3] The second Bank also suffered from incompetent leadership.

After the Supreme Court case, Maryland tried to prosecute McCulloch and his friends, but found a roadblock almost immediately. Embezzlement did not appear to be a crime! For hundreds of years, economies had been based on farming. The laws concerned themselves with the kinds of things that might go wrong on a farm. The new economy, based on free enterprise, had developed so quickly that the law had not caught up yet. In short, stealing an object that someone else has is clearly stealing. Stealing something that belongs to someone else but that the thief already has—the deposits in the Bank of the United States—was a new problem.[4]

Continued Hostility

The Supreme Court's decision in *McCulloch* settled the Bank's legal right to exist. It did nothing, however, to decrease the hostility toward it in Maryland. In regard to the other misdealings, after two trials, the Maryland courts refused to convict James McCulloch and his two partners of anything criminal. As one historian has explained, "Though the Maryland laws were evidently found wanting, it is probable that the [Maryland] court would have found [McCulloch and his partners] guilty [if] the injured party had not been the federal Bank. It joined instead the popular clamor and found the Bank guilty."[5] In other words, it said it was just too bad if the Bank of the United States had problems. It would not convict anyone of harming the Bank, especially with actions the law had never treated as being criminal.

Despite the Bank's problems, the efforts of newer leaders helped it fulfill most of Congress's hopes for it. The Bank continued to help regulate the money supply by printing paper money in exchange for gold and silver coins. Unfortunately, the Bank's leaders had a hard time figuring out how much paper money it should issue. Many people still believed that the printed paper money increased the actual amount of wealth. This was a mistake. Increasing the supply of money makes it easier to transfer wealth, for example, by buying and selling, paying taxes, or taking out and repaying loans. But it does not increase the amount of wealth. Only a growing economy can do that.[6]

Ultimately, the Bank did print too much paper money in an effort to support a growing economy. Many people blamed the Bank for an economic crisis in the late 1820s and early 1830s. The Bank's overenthusiasm in issuing banknotes certainly did not help, but there were many other causes of the crisis. Even so, President Andrew Jackson refused to approve the new charter that Congress passed in 1832. He vetoed it and continued to block efforts by those members of Congress who wanted to keep the Bank operating. The Bank's charter expired in 1837, and it went out of business.[7]

Money Without a Central Bank

Without a single central bank controlling currency, state-chartered banks again became the only place to exchange paper money and coins. However, these state-chartered banks could not, and did not, issue "legal tender" that could be used to make any payment. Instead, the paper money was just a statement of ownership of coins somewhere (very similar to checks written now). This made business dealings difficult outside the large cities. Since the paper money could be exchanged only at that bank, banks outside the large cities did not want to accept paper money from far away. The banks in the large cities, though, knew each other better. This tended to drive cities apart, because the bankers in each city trusted only the other bankers they knew personally. They did not trust bankers from far away. So they would not honor banknotes from far away. They only honored banknotes from bankers they personally knew.

To play up these advantages, some banks purposely

located themselves in hard-to-reach places. Others moved often. Although this does not sound like much of a problem now, the fact that paper money was not legal tender meant that Bank A did not have to accept paper money issued by Bank B. Often, they did not. During the 1850s, there were up to seven thousand different kinds of paper money circulating in the United States, backed by different banks. None were exchangeable everywhere.[8]

The National Banking Act

The *McCulloch* v. *Maryland* case had only temporarily changed banking in the United States. The Civil War changed it forever. Although the states that formed the Confederacy still distrusted the idea of a central bank, the northern states that stayed in the Union found chaos unacceptable.

In addition, having so many different kinds of paper money made counterfeiting easy. Indeed, the Confederates soon discovered this. In the Union in 1863, the National Banking Act made a single bank system the only authorized issuer of paper money. This helped control not only the currency supply but also the war effort. Since the system had only one design for money, recognizing counterfeit money was much easier. Having a central system also allowed Congress the flexibility to buy military supplies without transporting coins. Individual banks could still issue paper money, but only when approved by the central system. The form of the money also had to be approved by the central system.[9] The National Banking Act created an even stronger system than the Bank of the United States, even though it was divided among several banks.

The next forty years saw many significant developments in the United States' economy. Widespread railroads and powerful railroad barons emerged. The country's merchants, from shopkeepers and factory owners to shipmasters and traders, expanded to both coasts—and almost everywhere in between.

The National Banking Act's system still left most control in the hands of the national banks. Financial speculators, such as J. P. Morgan, began buying these banks, and using the deposits at the banks for their own schemes. This was not quite as disastrous as James McCulloch's misuse of funds in 1817. However, the "Panic of 1907" convinced even the bankers that the central banking system needed to be stronger.[10]

The Federal Reserve Bank of the United States

In 1913, the Federal Reserve Act established the Federal Reserve Bank of the United States. This strong system regulates the money supply of the country by ensuring that banks keep enough "real money" as deposits that they can cover any payments they must make. Since paper money was now as "real" as coins, this did not require keeping coins (gold or silver) in the bank. Instead, a bank must maintain a reserve based on the amount of money it has loaned out.

J. P. Morgan was one of the greatest financiers in the United States.

The Federal Reserve Bank changes the amount of this reserve to help control the growth in the money supply. The Federal Reserve also works closely with the Department of the Treasury to determine how much paper money and how many coins should be made.[11] This helps make sure that the value of money does not change too quickly. Money does wear out and needs to be replaced. If too much more is printed or minted compared to the economy's growth, each dollar becomes worth less. If too little is printed or minted compared to the economy's growth, each dollar becomes worth more, which quickly slows further growth.

The Federal Reserve system is not perfect. No bank is. There have still been economic crises, such as the Great Depression of the 1930s. The money supply is not the *only* thing that affects the overall economy. It is still an important part, though.

If the *McCulloch* decision had gone the other way, the second Bank of the United States would have closed immediately. It is impossible to tell what effect this might have on the United States today. The only thing that is certain is that the economy would be very, very different if the individual states had gained control of the nation's money. When the Bank's charter did expire later, it did so on schedule, in an orderly way. This allowed investors to get their money back. If the Bank had been forced to close immediately (if the *McCulloch* case had been decided against it), the financial problems of the 1820s and 1830s would have been much, much worse.

State Taxation of Federal Organizations

The *McCulloch* decision left the Bank of the United States in operation, at least for a while longer. It also said that states could not tax a federal organization. Although the Bank of the United States no longer exists, it is an important ancestor of the system of banking in place today. Chief Justice Marshall's theory on state taxation of federal organizations, however, has not withstood the test of time as strongly.

Chief Justice Marshall was faced with a tax that discriminated against the Bank. The Maryland tax was an attempt by one sovereign government (Maryland) to destroy a lawful act taken by another sovereign government (the United States). Marshall's opinion is not limited to just these discriminatory taxes, though. He reached beyond the facts of the case to make a broad statement prohibiting *any* tax by the states on *anything* done by the federal government. This was whether that tax discriminated against the federal government. He admitted that a state could tax real property (land and buildings) owned by the Bank, as long as it treated the Bank's real property the same as everyone else's.[12] But he denied the state's right to tax any *operation* of the Bank.

Since that time, the law on state taxation of federal operations has changed a great deal. Sometimes Congress specifically allows the states to tax its operations. For example, states may now tax national banks that participate in the Federal Reserve system.[13] Yet, Congress may specifically prohibit state taxation of certain operations.[14]

For a long time, states could not tax federal employees on their incomes. Likewise, the federal government could not tax state employees on their incomes.[15] The Supreme Court began changing its mind in the 1930s. First, it allowed the federal government to tax state employees. The next year, it allowed states to tax federal employees.[16] The Court also allowed taxes on land leased from governments and on construction contracts with the government.[17] The Court still does not allow taxes on one government by another, though. For example, if a contractor buys lumber for a federal government project, it must pay state sales tax on the lumber, because the tax is actually on the contractor, not the federal government.[18] However, if the contractor is acting only as an agent for the federal government, the state may not charge the sales tax. For example, a contractor who buys tractors to do a specific job, and must give the tractors to the federal government when the job is complete, does not have to pay sales tax on those tractors.[19]

Taxing power has expanded to include sales taxes on operations that do not have a strong relationship to sovereignty. New York used to sell mineral water at some of its state parks. At that time, there was a federal tax on the sale of mineral waters that applied to everyone. The Supreme Court said that the state had to pay the sales tax. Similarly, a city park district had to pay a federal admissions tax to use part of a federal forest. In contrast, it is still hard for states to tax federal activities, even though it is possible. The state taxes must be very general. They may only include activities that are not usually done by the federal government.[20]

Marshall's analysis is still valid in one very important area: government-issued bonds. Raising revenue is one of the core functions of any power.[21] Certainly, governments must have the money to pay for the services they provide. One of the most popular ways for governments to raise money is to sell bonds. A bond is very similar to a bank loan. The person who buys a bond loans the cost of the bond to the government. In return, the government promises to repay that money at a specific time in the future, usually in ten to thirty years. The government also promises to pay interest to the bondholder, just like someone who borrows money from a bank to buy a car pays interest to the bank.

Governments from cities and school districts all the way up to the federal government sell trillions of dollars worth of bonds to finance their activities. For example, outstanding bonds totaled over $19 trillion in the United States in late 2001. Federal bonds were worth about $4 trillion of this total. In comparison, the total value of all the stocks traded on the New York Stock Exchange at the end of 2001 was just under $12 trillion.[22] Because raising revenue is such an important function for any government, it is unconstitutional for a state to tax federal bonds, or for the federal government to tax state bonds. State bonds may also include bonds issued by cities and school districts, because cities and school districts fall under the state's sovereignty.[23]

Financial Regulation

As important as banks are, they are no longer the most important part of the money system. Most of the money that fuels the economy now comes from stocks and bonds, which together are called *securities.* In a matter of months, the Stock Market Crash of 1929 caused over a third of the combined value of American corporations to disappear. This disaster showed that securities were just as vulnerable to speculators as banks. The public simply would not participate in the securities markets unless it could trust that a James McCulloch, William Jones, J. P. Morgan, or other speculator would not manipulate the securities markets.

Most securities manipulation results from one of two kinds of schemes. One kind is similar to what James McCulloch did to the Bank of the United States. It happens when managers or major owners of securities force the company that issued the securities to operate for their benefit, instead of for the benefit of all of the owners. For example, a stockholder might use his ownership to give himself a job at the corporation, then embezzle from the company or take business for himself that should go to the corporation.[24] The other kind of manipulation happens when people who know company secrets, called "insiders," help some people buy and sell securities to make a profit based on those secrets.[25]

Before the Stock Market Crash in 1929, the states were unable to regulate securities to prevent these (and many other) abuses. They had adopted the so-called "blue sky" approach, trying to judge the actual soundness of corporations one by one. This was an attempt to prevent "speculative schemes that have no more basis than so many feet of blue sky."[26] There were no uniform standards, though. For example, the rules in New York were vastly different from those in Kansas. Having each state try to regulate all the securities sold to its citizens was an enormous task that, more often than not, simply was not done.

The Stock Market Crash of 1929 forced the federal government to act. The Securities Act of 1933 and Securities Exchange Act of 1934 rejected the "blue sky" approach of having the government judge the value of investments. Instead, they adopted a "disclosure" theory. This theory says that the public is smart enough to make those decisions—*if* it gets all of the information it needs to decide. These laws are important because they are national in scope, to help regulate a national economy. They are also important because it is possible to regulate the amount and kind of information that corporations disclose. The burden of judging whether those investments are also good ones is too much for the government to accept.[27]

Just how important these laws regulating securities can

be became clear in the late 1980s. Many savings and loan banks had invested in "junk bonds." These are very high-risk bonds that pay high interest to try to make it worth taking that risk. Unfortunately, these bonds were often pushed on them by Michael Milken, a trader at the securities broker Drexel Burnham Lambert, and his associates. The bonds were disasters for the savings and loans industries. One by one, the savings and loans began to go bankrupt. The problem was that Milken and his associates were manipulating the securities markets both by insider trading and by operating companies for their own benefit. Milken and his associates, including traders Ivan Boesky and Martin Siegel, were convicted of violating the securities laws and sentenced to prison. Without these laws, though, it is entirely possible that they would have gotten away with their crimes, which added up to well over $10 billion in theft and deception.[28]

McCulloch laid the foundation for the growth of the American economy by affirming the federal government's right to flexibly control the nation's money supply and financial systems. If the Bank had been found either unconstitutional or within Maryland's power to tax out of existence, bank regulation and the stock and bond markets, for example, would have been impossible.

8

The Decision and Federal Power

McCulloch v. *Maryland* is still one of the most-cited Supreme Court opinions.[1] The opinion has affected a lot more than just the Bank of the United States, too. Chief Justice Marshall made the concept of "implied powers" one that everyone would rely upon. He also reinforced that the federal government could rule supreme in the areas in which it is allowed to act.

Implied Powers

As discussed in Chapter 6, Chief Justice Marshall found two different ways that the Constitution gives the federal government implied powers.[2] Alexander Hamilton's argument that giving a power necessarily gives the means to execute that power is itself an "implied power." This theory would have been enough support to rule that Congress had the power to charter the Bank. The Constitution grants Congress the power to "coin Money, regulate the Value thereof, and of foreign Coin" and to "provide for the Punishment of counterfeiting the Securities and current Coin of the United States."[3] As Hamilton had argued in 1791, and as Daniel Webster and William Pinkney argued in 1819, this is enough by itself. Establishing a bank to exchange coins and money, hold deposits, make loans, and convert between foreign and American money is one way to "regulate the value" of money, both American and foreign.

The Risks

Although this is an important theory, it carries two risks. First, it does not help explain the limits of any particular power. Banking seems closely related to regulating currency. Some of the other powers granted to Congress are much less clear, especially as technology changes. For example, the Constitution authorizes Congress to maintain an army and a navy, but it does not authorize Congress to maintain an air force. Defining air power as a part of either the army or navy is one solution. However, by the end of World War II, air power was a separate resource for the military, at least equal to armies and navies. Relying just on implied powers within a single granted power would not cover this possibility.[4]

Second, relying only on the means to execute granted powers as a source of implied powers carries another risk. It does not help understand an implied power's limits when it might have more than one source in the Constitution. For example, Congress can "establish Post Offices and Post Roads."[5] It can give inventors the "exclusive Right . . . for limited Times." Which of these clauses would apply to a telegraph or telephone system? Both the telephone and the telegraph were inventions. They also acted as substitutes for the essential function of post offices and post roads: delivery of messages over distances.[6]

Marshall's interpretation of the Necessary and Proper Clause answers all these objections. If an act of the federal government is, in Congress's judgment, necessary and proper to exercise one of the powers granted to the federal government, it is constitutional under the Necessary and Proper Clause unless it is otherwise prohibited. Therefore, establishing an air force is necessary and proper to continue maintaining an effective army and navy. Likewise, setting standards for how telephone and telegraph systems must operate is necessary and proper to continue maintaining a system of post offices and post roads in light of advancing technology. At the same time, those standards allow inventors of telegraph and telephone equipment to continue to have exclusive rights to their inventions.[7]

Limited Power

Marshall had made sure that the federal government would have the power to do what is "necessary and proper."

However, not all courts—even later Justices of the Supreme Court—agreed that this was a broad and sweeping power. For a century after Marshall's death in 1836, the Supreme Court stayed very skeptical of any federal action not directly related to one of the seventeen specific grants of power in Article I, section 8 of the Constitution, or to regulating the money supply. Most justices believed that the states should do just about everything. They tried very hard to find reasons elsewhere in the Constitution to restrict federal action.

The most famous of these restrictions was the doctrine of *substantive due process.* Judges often overturned laws that, even though they appeared to be in line with *McCulloch,* restricted other rights. The Contract Clause of the Constitution was the most common authority for overturning these laws. The Contract Clause prohibits states from enacting laws *impairing,* changing the terms of, contracts.[8] This was often used to prevent government regulation of health or working conditions, on the ground that these restrictions "impaired" the contracts between workers and companies. The most famous of these cases was *Lochner* v. *New York,* a 1905 decision. *Lochner* overruled a New York law that prohibited companies from forcing bakers to work more than sixty hours in a week, or ten hours in any day. Even though the New York law was intended to reduce the injuries to bakers caused by working such long hours, the Supreme Court held that the law "impaired" the natural contracts between bakers and baking companies.[9]

The Power to Act When Needed

During the Great Depression of the 1930s, though, the federal government was the only organization able to act to help the millions of unemployed workers and their families. In 1937, the Supreme Court overruled *Lochner* and allowed the federal government to use its powers under the Commerce Clause to justify regulations that might affect some contracts.[10] The *Commerce Clause* gives Congress the power to "regulate Commerce…among the several States." In *West Coast Hotel Co.* v. *Parrish*, the Supreme Court ruled that Washington State could set a minimum wage for women.[11] A few months later, the Court allowed the federal government to prohibit shipment between states of filled milk.[12] (*Filled milk* is watered down and then fortified with oils.) These 1930s opinions both depend on *McCulloch's* interpretation of the Necessary and Proper Clause. They made the powerful federal agencies that influence every aspect of life today possible.[13]

The Benefits

Chief Justice Marshall's interpretation of the Necessary and Proper Clause actually helps keep the courts out of the law-making process. Without this broad interpretation (explained in Chapter 6), every Congressional act not directly related to a literal power in the Constitution could be challenged. The courts would have to determine for each individual law whether it was close enough to the

Constitution's grant of powers. However, Chief Justice Marshall's opinion means that if "it would be reasonable for the Congress to view the problem as connected to one of the Constitution's grants of power, the law will be upheld [by the courts], unless Congress's power is limited by the Bill of Rights or other specific provisions."[14]

Perhaps most importantly, though, Congress actually can act. Before *McCulloch*, if a law Congress was considering passing did not virtually quote a clause in Article I, Section 8, it had to debate whether the law was within its power. *McCulloch* gave Congress the freedom to shape laws to meet particular needs, especially needs that were clearly related to one of its powers from Section 8. *McCulloch* and the Necessary and Proper Clause were combined with the Commerce Clause in the 1930s to allow the federal government to regulate a nation—and its economy—that increasingly ignored state lines and state traditions.[15]

Everything in Balance

In addition, the Necessary and Proper Clause does not give the federal government unlimited power. The Constitution forces the federal government to share power between the branches of government. Control of foreign affairs is shared between Congress and the president. For example, both Congress and the president must cooperate to make a treaty. The president can negotiate a treaty, but the treaty does not become effective until ratified by two-thirds of the Senate.[16]

Once a treaty has been made, the Necessary and Proper Clause gives Congress the power to pass all laws needed to implement the treaty. For example, Congress could pass laws to implement a treaty between the United States and Canada to protect birds that migrate between the two countries. Even though states usually determine what kind of hunting is legal, Congress could prohibit hunting these birds. This may happen even though there is nothing in the Constitution that specifically says anything about birds or hunting. The Tenth Amendment does not bar Congress from fulfilling this duty. Congress can pass laws to support a treaty with another country to protect birds that migrate between the countries. It is "necessary and proper" that Congress has the power, even though the Tenth Amendment seems to save so much power for the states and people.[17]

Congress and the president share other powers and roles in foreign relations. For example, Congress must provide all money for the president to take action. If it chooses, Congress can prevent the president from doing something it does not approve of by prohibiting use of funds for that purpose. For example, when Congress disagreed with President Ronald Reagan's policies in Central America during the 1980s, it passed a law that prohibited use of any federal money supporting those policies.[18]

The Supreme Law of the Land

Chief Justice Marshall's use of the Supremacy Clause to invalidate the Maryland law was not popular or quickly accepted. The Bank of the United States continued to be the target of attacks by states. Questions about it ended up back in the Supreme Court only a few years after *McCulloch*. For example, Ohio had passed a law directing its auditor to seize a tax "from all banks and individuals, and companies and associations of individuals, that may transact business in this state without being allowed to do so by the laws thereof." The Bank, not having an Ohio charter, was not allowed to transact business by Ohio law. The state's auditor, Ralph Osborn, seized $100,000 from the Bank's branch in Chillicothe, Ohio. After two years of negotiations, a federal court ordered Ohio to return the money. Ohio refused, so federal agents put the auditor in prison.[19]

In *Osborn* v. *Bank of the United States* in 1824, Chief Justice Marshall and the Supreme Court ruled that the Ohio taxes were invalid, both under the *McCulloch* decision and the Supremacy Clause itself. They also ruled that the order of the federal court must be obeyed by Ohio, even though Ohio's legislature had passed its own law. Although this would not be the last of the lawsuits involving the Bank of the United States in its remaining years, it was the last one that seriously threatened the Bank itself. Although the Bank of the United States was named as a party in the lawsuit, the Bank's participation seemed almost meaningless by the time the case was heard by the Supreme Court. Ohio's anger by that time focussed on the authority of the federal court to order the arrest of its auditor.[20]

The most serious challenges to the Supremacy Clause since the end of the Civil War have come in civil rights cases. At times, these challenges have been violent. Many states, particularly those in the South, passed laws to enforce racial discrimination during the years after the Civil War. These laws, often called "Jim Crow laws," became even more common after the Supreme Court's 1896 decision in *Plessy* v. *Ferguson* that allowed states to enforce segregation. In 1954, the Supreme Court overruled *Plessy* in the first of the two *Brown v. Board of Education* decisions.[21]

This, however, did not end the Southern states' resistance to integration. Despite specific rulings from several federal courts, some states refused to integrate their schools. This nearly resulted in fighting between the Arkansas state militia and soldiers in the U.S. Army. Governor Orville Faubus had sent state militia troops to the Little Rock, Arkansas, schools to keep African-American children from attending "white" schools. The Supreme Court took the matter very seriously. All nine justices signed an opinion telling Governor Faubus that he could not defy the Supreme Court. Supreme Court rulings cannot be *evaded*, or avoided, either "openly and directly by state legislators or state executive or judicial officers" or "indirectly by them through evasive schemes." President Dwight D. Eisenhower sent soldiers to the schools to escort African-American children into the classrooms.[22]

One argument some supporters of segregation made was that *Brown* and desegregation could be right only if the Supremacy Clause completely eliminates the role of states in constitutional law. This is incorrect. For example, the Constitution mandates several rights for criminal defendants, such as the right to counsel and the right to silence.[23] If the Supreme Court determines that there is no *federal*

In order to enforce the decision to desegregate schools, President Eisenhower had to send soldiers to Arkansas schools to escort African-American children to the classrooms.

guarantee of a right to counsel in every criminal case, that does not prevent a state from supplying that right in its own courts (even if a federal court in that state does not have to follow the state's rule). States may also anticipate that the U.S. Supreme Court may later decide that the Constitution does guarantee such a right.[24] This leaves an important role for the states to play. Chief Justice Marshall's opinion in *McCulloch* made clear that that the states could continue to give their citizens *more* rights and privileges than the federal government does, so long as there is no conflict. The Supremacy Clause only matters when there is a conflict. When there is no conflict, the states are free to interpret their own laws as they wish.[25]

A Strong, But Limited, Federal Government

Chief Justice Marshall's opinion in *McCulloch* laid the foundation for a strong federal government. As one scholar has remarked:

> [T]he judicial role was to Marshall a means, not an end. [He used] his independence to mold the law in accordance with the needs of American society . . . . [His] goal was to lay down constitutional principles that would give effect to [his] vision . . . and both protect property rights and their expansion to permit them to be used to foster the growing [free enterprise] economy.[26]

In other words, Marshall was much less interested in how much power he could get as a Justice than how he could use the power he had to help the United States grow and continue to grow after his death. He believed that this required a strong national government with all the necessary powers to build an ever-larger nation.

The federal government still has limits, however. Although *McCulloch* does allow the federal government a great deal of flexibility in applying its powers, it does not actually expand the powers of the federal government. Such an expansion can come only from amending the Constitution.[27] The dynamic government today exists because the Bank of the United States defended itself, and therefore defended the power of the federal government, despite the thievery of James McCulloch himself. Although in other incidents McCulloch stole from the Bank, in a way, he gave the young nation back a great deal more than he took.

Chapter Notes

Chapter 1. A Visit to the Bank

1. Bray Hammond, "The Bank Cases," John A. Garraty, ed., *Quarrels That Have Shaped the Constitution*, rev. ed. (New York: Harper & Row, 1987), p. 37.

2. Ibid., pp. 37–38.

3. Ibid., pp. 41–43.

4. Arthur Nussbaum, *A History of the Dollar* (New York: Columbia University Press, 1957), p. 11.

5. Hammond, pp. 40–41.

6. Ibid., pp. 37–39.

7. The Articles of Confederation, which were in effect between the end of the Revolutionary War in 1776 and the ratification of the Constitution in 1789, specifically allowed each state to have these powers.

8. Nussbaum, pp. 1–34, 37–42.

9. Ibid., pp. 24–42.

10. *Marbury v. Madison*, 5 U.S. 137 (1803); John E. Nowak and Ronald D. Rotunda, *Constitutional Law*, 4th ed. (St. Paul, Minn.: West Publishing, 1991), pp. 3–9, 13–17.

11. U.S. Constitution, Art. III, § 2, cl.2; Judiciary Act of 1789, § 25; *Federalist Papers,* No. 82 (Hamilton).

12. *Fletcher v. Peck*, 10 U.S. 87 (1810).

13. Nowak and Rotunda, pp. 14–16.

14. U.S. Constitution, Art. I, § 8.

15. Ibid., Art. I, § 8, cl. 18.

16. *McCulloch v. Maryland,* 17 U.S. 317, 317–319 (1819).

Chapter 2. The Money Game

1. Bray Hammond, *Banks and Politics in America: From the Revolution to the Civil War* (Princeton, N.J.: Princeton University Press, 1957), pp. 40–48.

2. Ibid., pp. 48–50.

3. Ibid., pp. 50–64.

4. Compare to Hammond, pp. 69–70, 77–85.

5. Arthur Nussbaum, *A History of the Dollar* (New York: Columbia University Press, 1957), p. 44–46.

6. Hammond, pp. 114–18; Nussbaum, pp. 49–51.

7. Hammond, pp. 172–188.

8. Hammond, pp. 214–226; Nussbaum, pp. 69–71.

9. Nussbaum, p. 70.

10. Ibid., pp. 70–71.

11. John A. Garraty and Peter Gay, eds., *The Columbia History of the World* (New York: Harper & Row, 1967), pp. 796–797.

12. Hammond, pp. 233–250.

13. Bray Hammond, "The Bank Cases," John A. Garraty, ed., *Quarrels That Have Shaped the Constitution,* rev. ed. (New York: Harper & Row, 1987), pp. 37–41.

14. Hammond, *Banks and Politics in America: From the Revolution to the Civil War,* p. 264.

15. Calculated from historical indices available at <http://www.orst.edu/Dept/pol_sci/fac/sahr/sahr.htm> (adjusted for population); John Maynard Keynes, *A Treatise on Money,* vol. I (London: Macmillan, 1930), pp. 53–64.

16. Hammond, *Banks and Politics in America: From the Revolution to the Civil War,* pp. 227–241, 246–250, 260–262.

17. Ibid., pp. 251–253, 260–263.

18. Ibid., pp. 268–271.

Chapter 3. Sharing Power

1. William H. Rehnquist, *The Supreme Court,* new ed. (New York: Knopf, 2001), p. 21.

2. Charles Grove Haines, *The Role of the Supreme Court in American Government and Politics, 1789–1935* (Berkeley, Calif.: University of California Press, 1944), pp. 52–82; Leonard Baker, *John Marshall: A Life in Law* (New York: Macmillan, 1974), pp. 22–38, 107–118.

3. *London Gazette,* April 8–11, 1775.

4. Articles of Confederation, Art. III.

5. Ibid., Art. IX, cl. 2.

6. Ibid., Art. VI–IX.

7. Ibid., Art. VI, IX.

8. Haines, pp. 85–105; Bray Hammond, *Banks and Politics in America: From the Revolution to the Civil War* (Princeton, N.J.: Princeton University Press, 1957), pp. 52–81.

9. Articles of Confederation, Art. IX, cl. 4.

10. Hammond, pp. 46–64.

11. U.S. Constitution, Art. I–III.

12. Ibid., Art. VI cl.2, Art. I § 8, § 9.

13. Michael Kamen, *A Machine That Would Go of Itself* (New York: Knopf, 1985), pp. 41–52, 185–216.

14. U.S. Constitution, Art. III, § 1; Judiciary Act of 1789.

15. Kermit Hall, ed., *The Oxford Companion to the Supreme Court* (New York: Oxford University Press, 1992), p. 978.

16. *Marbury v. Madison*, 5 U.S. 137 (1803).

17. U.S. Constitution, Art. III, § 2.

18. John E. Nowak and Ronald D. Rotunda, *Constitutional Law*, 4th ed. (St. Paul, Minn.: West Publishing, 1991), pp. 3–9, 13–14.

Chapter 4. The Case for James McCulloch

1. Craig Joyce, "Wheaton, Henry," in ed. Kermit L. Hall, *The Oxford Companion to the Supreme Court* (New York: Oxford University Press, 1992), p. 926.

2. Maurice Baxter, "Webster, Daniel," in ed. Kermit L. Hall, *The Oxford Companion to the Supreme Court* (New York: Oxford University Press, 1992), p. 921.

3. *McCulloch v. Maryland*, 17 U.S. 322 (1819). The argument presented in the official report is Mr. Wheaton's summary of Mr. Webster's argument; it is not a transcript, such as one might find in court today.

4. U.S. Constitution, Art. I, § 8, cl. 18.

5. Ibid., Art. I, § 8, cl. 5.

6. *McCulloch v. Maryland*, 17 U.S. 323–324.

7. Glyn Davies, *A History of Money From Ancient Times to the Present Day* (Cardiff, UK: University of Wales Press, 1994), pp. 254–270.

8. U.S. Constitution, Art. I, § 8, cl. 11–13.

9. *McCulloch v. Maryland*, 17 U.S. 324–325.

10. U.S. Constitution, Amend. X.

11. *McCulloch v. Maryland,* 17 U.S. 324–326.

12. U.S. Constitution, Art. VI, cl. 2.

13. *McCulloch v. Maryland,* 17 U.S. 326–330.

14. Maurice Baxter, "Wirt, William," in ed. Kermit L. Hall, *The Oxford Companion to the Supreme Court* (New York: Oxford University Press, 1992), p. 934.

15. *McCulloch v. Maryland,* 17 U.S. 352–355 (quotation is the reporter's summary).

16. Compare U.S. Constitution, Art. I, § 8, cl. 13 with Art. I, § 9, cl.3.

17. *McCulloch v. Maryland,* 17 U.S. 354–360.

18. U.S. Constitution, Art. VI, cl. 2.

19. *McCulloch v. Maryland,* 17 U.S. 360–362.

20. *Martin v. Hunter's Lessee,* 14 U.S. 304 (1816); U.S. Constitution, Art. I, § 10, cl. 1.

21. U.S. Constitution, Amend. XI.

22. Maurice Baxter, "Pinkney, William," in ed. Kermit L. Hall, *The Oxford Companion to the Supreme Court* (New York: Oxford University Press, 1992), p. 635.

23. *McCulloch v. Maryland,* 17 U.S. 377–385.

24. U.S. Constitution, Art. I, § 8, cl. 18.

25. *McCulloch v. Maryland,* 17 U.S. 386–390.

26. Ibid., 17 U.S. 391 (quotation is the reporter's summary).

27. Ibid., 17 U.S. 391–400.

Chapter 5. The Case for Maryland

1. *McCulloch v. Maryland,* 17 U.S. 317, 330–331 (1819) (quotation is the reporter's summary).

2. U.S. Constitution, Art. I, § § 8–9.

3. Ibid., Art. I, § 8, cl. 4.

4. *Sturges v. Crowninshield,* 17 U.S. 122 (1819).

5. U.S. Constitution, Art. I, § 8, cl. 18; *McCulloch v. Maryland,* 17 U.S. at 331–33.

6. *McCulloch v. Maryland,* 17 U.S. 334–335.

7. Ibid., 17 U.S. 335–337.

8. Ibid., 17 U.S. 337–338 (quotation is the reporter's summary).

9. Ibid., 17 U.S. 338–344.

10. *Federalist Papers* No. 34 (Hamilton) <http://www.gutenberg.org>; *Antifederalist Papers* <http://www.logoplex.com/shops/leaders/afp.txt>.

11. U.S. Constitution, Art. I, § 10, cl. 2–3.

12. *McCulloch v. Maryland,* 17 U.S. 347–352.

13. Ibid., 17 U.S. 362–365.

14. Ibid., 17 U.S. 365 (quotation is the reporter's summary).

15. U.S. Constitution, Art. I, § 8, cl. 5.

16. *McCulloch v. Maryland,* 17 U.S. 366–367.

17. U.S. Constitution, Amend. X.

18. *Merriam-Webster's Collegiate Dictionary,* Deluxe Electronic Edition (Springfield, Mass.: Merriam-Webster, 1995).

19. U.S. Constitution, Art. I, § 10, cl. 2–3.

20. *McCulloch v. Maryland,* 17 U.S. 368–369.

21. Ibid., 17 U.S. 369–372.

22. U.S. Constitution, Art. VI, cl. 2.

23. *McCulloch v. Maryland*, 17 U.S. 372–374 (quotation is the reporter's summary).

24. Ibid., 17 U.S. 375.

25. Ibid., 17 U.S. 375–377. The short form of "Attorney General" is "General," just like the short form of "Lieutenant General" is also "General."

26. *Fairfax's Devisee v. Hunter's Lessee*, 11 U.S. 603 (1813); *Martin v. Hunter's Lessee*, 14 U.S. 304 (1816).

27. John E. Nowak and Ronald D. Rotunda, *Constitutional Law*, 4th ed. (St. Paul, Minn.: West Publishing, 1991), pp. 117–126; Laurence H. Tribe, *Constitutional Choices* (Cambridge, Mass.: Harvard University Press, 1985) pp. 9–20; Laurence H. Tribe and Michael C. Dorf, *On Reading the Constitution* (Cambridge, Mass.: Harvard University Press, 1991).

Chapter 6. The Decision

1. Francis N. Stites, *John Marshall: Defender of the Constitution* (Boston: Little, Brown, 1980), pp. 1–14.

2. Leonard Baker, *John Marshall: A Life in Law* (New York: Macmillan, 1974), pp. 70–73.

3. Charles F. Hobson, *The Great Chief Justice: John Marshall and the Rule of Law* (Lawrence, Kan.: University Press of Kansas, 1996), pp. 5–8.

4. William H. Rehnquist, *The Supreme Court*, new ed. (New York: Knopf, 2001), p. 43.

5. Baker, pp. 364–71; Stites, pp. 77–89.

6. *Marbury v. Madison*, 5 U.S. 137 (1803).

7. John E. Nowak and Ronald D. Rotunda, *Constitutional Law*, 4th ed. (St. Paul, Minn.: West Publishing, 1991), pp. 13–20.

8. *McCulloch v. Maryland,* 17 U.S. 316, 400 (1819) (beginning of Marshall's opinion).

9. Ibid., 17 U.S. 400–401.

10. Ibid., 17 U.S. 401–402.

11. Ibid., 17 U.S. 402–405.

12. U.S. Constitution, Art. VI, cl. 2; *McCulloch v. Maryland,* 17 U.S. 405–406.

13. U.S. Constitution, Amend. X.

14. *McCulloch v. Maryland,* 17 U.S. 406–407.

15. Ibid., 17 U.S. 408–414; U.S. Constitution, Art. I, § 8, cl. 18.

16. Ibid., 17 U.S. 414–417.

17. Ibid., 17 U.S. 417–425.

18. Ibid., 17 U.S. 425–429.

19. Ibid., 17 U.S. 427–437.

Chapter 7. The Decision and the Money System

1. *McCulloch v. Maryland,* 17 U.S. 437 (1819).

2. Ibid., 17 U.S. 316.

3. Federal Reserve *Bulletin,* Dec. 1999.

4. Bray Hammond, *Banks and Politics in America: From the Revolution to the Civil War* (Princeton, N.J.: Princeton University Press, 1957), pp. 227–241, 246–250, 260–262.

5. Ibid., pp. 268–271.

6. Hammond, p. 272.

7. Harry E. Miller, *Banking Theories in the United States Before 1860* (Cambridge, Mass.: Harvard University Press, 1927), pp. 39–44.

8. Hammond, pp. 354–371, 400–409; William W. Wade, *From Barter to Banking: The Story of Money* (New York: Crowell-Collier Press, 1967), pp. 58–59.

9. Wade, pp. 58–62; Hammond, pp. 685–695, 700–707.

10. Hammond, pp. 725–734.

11. Wade, pp. 62–71.

12. Ibid.

13. *McCulloch v. Maryland*, 17 U.S. 424–429.

14. 12 U.S.C. § 548 ("a national bank shall be treated as a bank organized and existing under the laws of the State or other jurisdiction within which its principal office is located").

15. *Carson v. Roane-Anderson Co.*, 342 U.S. 232 (1952).

16. *Dobbins v. Commissioners of Erie County*, 41 U.S. 435 (1842) (state income tax on federal employees is unconstitutional); *Collector v. Day*, 78 U.S. 113 (1871) (federal income tax on state judge is unconstitutional).

17. *Helvering v. Gerhardt*, 304 U.S. 405 (1938) (state agency employee); *Graves v. New York ex rel. O'Keefe*, 306 U.S. 466 (1939) (federal agency employee).

18. *United States v. County of Fresno*, 429 U.S. 452 (1977) (leased land); *Helvering v. Mountain Producers Corp.*, 303 U.S. 376 (1938) (leased land); *James v. Dravo Contracting Co.*, 302 U.S. 134 (1937) (contractors).

19. *Alabama v. King & Boozer*, 314 U.S. 1 (1941).

20. *Kern-Limerick, Inc. v. Scurlock*, 347 U.S. 110 (1954).

21. *New York v. United States,* 326 U.S. 572 (1946) (mineral waters); *Wilmette Park Dist. v. Campbell,* 338 U.S. 411 (1949) (admissions); *United States v. State Tax Commission,* 421 U.S. 599 (1975) (state taxes on federal activities).

22. U.S. Constitution, Art. I, § 8, cl. 5; *McCulloch v. Maryland,* 17 U.S.C. 407–409, 425–430.

23. *Flow of Funds Accounts of the United States* (Federal Reserve Statistical Release Z.1), Dec. 7, 2001, table D.3 at 8; New York Stock Exchange record for the month ending December 31, 2001, <http://www.nyse.com>.

24. *Miller v. Milwaukee,* 272 U.S. 713 (1927) (state may not tax federal bonds); *Pollock v. Farmers' Loan & Trust Co.,* 157 U.S. 429 (1895) (federal government may not tax state bonds).

25. William A. Klein and John C. Coffee, Jr., *Business Organization and Finance,* 5th ed. (Westbury, N.Y.: Foundation Press, 1993), pp. 163–171; Harold Marsh, Jr., "Are Directors Trustees? Conflicts of Interest and Corporate Morality," 22 *Business Lawyer* 35 (1966).

26. *Securities Exchange Comm'n v. Texas Gulf Sulphur Co.,* 401 F.2d 833 (2d Cir. 1968), *cert. denied,* 394 U.S. 976 (1969); *In re Cady Roberts & Co.,* 40 S.E.C. 907 (1961); Klein and Coffee, pp. 154–163.

27. *Hall v. Geiger-Jones Co.,* 242 U.S. 539, 550 (1917).

28. Securities Act of 1933, 15 U.S.C. § 77a; Securities Exchange Act of 1934, 15 U.S.C. § 78a.

Chapter 8. The Decision and Federal Power

1. James B. Stewart, *Den of Thieves* (New York: Simon & Schuster, 1991).

2. *McCulloch v. Maryland,* 17 U.S. 316 (1819).

3. U.S. Constitution, Art. I, § 8, cl. 5, 6; Bernard Schwartz, *A History of the Supreme Court* (New York: Oxford University Press, 1993), p. 46.

4. U.S. Constitution, Art. I, § 8, cl. 12, 13.

5. Ibid., Art. I, § 8, cl. 7, 8; *McCulloch v. Maryland,* 17 U.S. 417.

6. Ibid., Art. I, § 8, cl. 18; *McCulloch v. Maryland,* 17 U.S. 411–421.

7. Compare Schwartz, *History,* pp. 46–47.

8. U.S. Constitution, Art. I, § 10, cl. 1.

9. *Lochner v. New York,* 198 U.S. 45 (1905).

10. U.S. Constitution, Art. I, § 8, cl. 3.

11. *West Coast Hotel Co. v. Parrish,* 300 U.S. 379 (1937).

12. *United States v. Carolene Products Co.,* 304 U.S. 144 (1938).

13. John E. Nowak and Ronald D. Rotunda, *Constitutional Law,* 4th ed. (St. Paul, Minn.: West Publishing, 1991), pp. 371–380.

14. Ibid., p. 121.

15. *United States v. Carolene Products Co.,* 304 U.S. 144.

16. U.S. Constitution, Art. II, § 2, cl. 1.

17. *Missouri v. Holland,* 252 U.S. 416 (1920); U.S. Constitution, Amend. X (1791).

18. This is commonly called the "Boland Amendment," after Congressman Edward Boland of Massachusetts who proposed it. Pub. L. 98–215 (1983) (H.R. 98–2968, Amend. 416); Nowak and Rotunda, pp. 201–205.

19. Bray Hammond, "The Bank Cases," John A. Garraty, ed., *Quarrels That Have Shaped the Constitution*, rev. ed. (New York: Harper & Row, 1987), pp. 47–51.

20. *Osborn v. Bank of the United States*, 22 U.S. 738 (1824).

21. *Plessy v. Ferguson*, 163 U.S. 537 (1896), *overruled by Brown v. Board of Education*, 347 U.S. 483 (1954).

22. *Cooper v. Aaron*, 358 U.S. 1, 17 (1958).

23. U.S. Constitution, Amend. VI (1791), V (1791).

24. *Carpenter v. County of Dane*, 9 Wis. 249 (1859).

25. *McCulloch v. Maryland*, 17 U.S. 426; Justice William J. Brennan, "State Constitutions and the Protection of Individual Rights," 90 *Harvard Law Review* 489 (1977).

26. Bernard Schwartz, *A History of the Supreme Court* (New York: Oxford University Press, 1993), p. 67.

27. To date, the only such amendment that directly increases federal power is U.S. Const. Amend. XVI (1913) (giving Congress the power to collect a tax on personal incomes). Several other amendments give Congress power to enforce new rights they grant; *e.g.,* U.S. Const., Amend. XIV § 5 (1868).

Glossary

ambassador—The highest official representative of a another nation.

auditor—An accountant who checks a company's accounting records to ensure that they are correct.

bank—An organization that stores and exchanges money to make trade more efficient.

banknotes—Paper money, such as dollar bills, that is issued for general purposes. A banknote has a preprinted value on it.

briefs—Arguments written by lawyers that are presented to a court.

capital—Products and things that may be exchanged for other products and things. In modern use, this mainly means paper money and other things valued like money.

capitalization—The value of a corporation's stock. Modern large corporations calculate capitalization from stock-market value. Older and smaller corporations calculate capitalization from the amount of money their stock is worth at the beginning.

cashier—A person who handles money. In a bank, the cashier is an officer of the bank who may supervise tellers (other people who actually deal with customers).

central bank—A bank or government agency that regulates currency and the money supply of a nation. The Federal Reserve is the central bank in the United States.

central government—A national government that has great control over governments under it, such as states, counties, and cities.

chaos—State of confusion.

charter—The government's permission for a corporation to exist.

Commerce Clause—"The Congress shall have Power . . . to regulate Commerce with foreign Nations, and among the several States, and with the Indian Tribes." U.S. Constitution, Art. I, § 8, cl. 3.

corporation—A business in which several (or many) people pool their money, in return for shares of ownership. Corporations must be specifically chartered by a government.

counterfeit—An unauthorized imitation of real money.

credit—An acknowledgment that someone will pay in the future for something he purchases now.

currency—Money that actually changes hands when things are sold. Sometimes called "cash," it includes both coins and banknotes.

defendant in error—The party that won the decision in the lower court; now called "appellee."

director—A policy-setting officer of a corporation appointed or elected by the owners.

doctrine—A formally established way of thinking or doing things.

embezzle—When someone who has been trusted to handle money for a company or person steals it from that company or person.

enumerated powers—A specific list of powers given to the federal government in the U.S. constitution that implies that anything not listed is not authorized.

exclusive—Sole, single; belonging only to one person or group.

face value—The amount of money that a coin or banknote says it is worth. For example, a one-dollar bill has a face value of one dollar, even though as a piece of paper with ink on it is worth a lot less than one cent.

Federalism—A government in which the central government shares power with governments under it, such as states. The central government usually has the last say in arguments.

foreclosed—Calling in a loan for immediate repayment. Many loans are secured (guaranteed) by the value of a piece of property. In a foreclosure, the bank will seize this property because the loan was not repaid.

free enterprise—An economic system based on individual businesspeople deciding how to run their businesses to gain the greatest profit.

impair—To change terms in a contract, or prevent someone from enforcing part or all of a contract.

import duties—Taxes paid on goods imported from another country.

integration—The process of eliminating barriers.

judiciary—An organized system of judges and courts established to resolve disputes between private citizens, to try criminal cases, and to interpret the laws.

Justice—The title of a judge.

legal tender—Money that can be used to pay any debt. Early paper money was not legal tender; the person or government who was owed the money could demand to be paid in coins.

mint—A place that the government authorizes to make money (usually coins, but sometimes banknotes, as well).

monopoly—Exclusive possession or control. When one company is the only one that can do a certain kind of business, it has a monopoly on that business.

Necessary and Proper Clause—"The Congress shall have Power . . . to make all Laws which shall be necessary and proper for carrying into Execution the foregoing Powers, and all other Powers vested by this Constitution in the Government of the United States, or any Department or Officer thereof." U.S. Constitution, Art. I, § 8, cl. 18.

plaintiff in error—The party filing an appeal; now called "appellant."

promissory note—A promise to pay a sum of money at a specific time in the future.

ratify—To formally agree with a decision or action.

recession—A time when the economy is shrinking, not growing. A severe, long-term recession may become a depression, like the Great Depression of the 1930s.

scheme—A plan, usually illegal.

securities—Financial documents, like stocks and bonds, that are used to raise money for corporations and governments instead of bank loans.

segregation—Enforced separation, especially for racial reasons.

shareholders—People who own shares, or parts of, a corporation, and have the right to vote on corporation management.

sovereign—The person or organization that has independent, governmental power.

sovereignty—The right of a government to rule without interference from another government. The American colonies were not "sovereigns," because their governments were controlled by the English Parliament. However, the individual states were sovereigns under the Articles of Confederation, because their governments were not really controlled by the Articles.

stamp—Proof that a tax or other government fee has been paid; postage stamps, for example, are proof that the cost of sending an item has been paid.

States' Rights—The belief that the Constitution is an agreement between the states that signed it, and that the states therefore are independent.

substantive due process—A theory that overturns laws that limit rights or liberties that were believed to be guaranteed by other basic and natural rights.

Supremacy Clause—"This Constitution, and the Laws of the United States which shall be made in Pursuance thereof; and all Treaties made, or which shall be made, under the Authority of the United States, shall be the supreme Law of the Land; and the Judges in every State shall be bound thereby, any Thing in the Constitution or Laws of any State to the Contrary notwithstanding." U.S. Constitution, Art. VI, cl. 2.

writ of error—Procedure used at the time of *McCulloch* to appeal a lower court's decision.

Further Reading

Aaseng, Nathan. *Great Justices of the Supreme Court.* Minneapolis, Minn.: The Oliver Press, Inc., 1992.

Baum, Lawrence. *The Supreme Court.* Washington, D.C.: Congressional Quarterly, Inc., 2000.

DeVillers, David. *Marbury v. Madison: Powers of the Supreme Court.* Berkeley Heights, N.J.: Enslow Publishers, Inc., 1998.

Nardo, Don. *The U.S. Constitution.* Farmington Hills, Mich.: Gale Group, 2001.

Weidner, Daniel W. *Constitution: The Preamble and the Articles.* Berkeley Heights, N.J.: Enslow Publishers, Inc., 2002.

Internet Addresses

InfoPlease.com: The Supreme Court

Get the facts about the Supreme Court Justices, the history of their decisions, milestone cases, and more.

<http://www.infoplease.com/ipa/A0873869.html>

TeenGov

Find out about the political powers regular people have in the United States. Includes facts about the Supreme Court, state governments, Congress, and the president.

<http://www.teengov.org>

Index